Memoirs Of An Ordinary Man

A Yorkshireman's Tale

Aaron Chynn

authorHOUSE®

AuthorHouse™ UK Ltd.
500 Avebury Boulevard
Central Milton Keynes, MK9 2BE
www.authorhouse.co.uk
Phone: 08001974150

First published by AuthorHouse 9/3/2009

ISBN: 978-1-4389-9399-7 (sc)

This book is printed on acid-free paper.

PREFACE

If you are expecting a life story then this is not it, nor is it a diary, it is a collection of accounts of true events, not in any order, the only connection between one event and another is the fact that they are absolutely true and either happened to me, or whilst I was there. Only the names, dates and events have been changed to protect the author from anyone wielding baseball bats, therefore with a bit of luck, any resemblance between this book and the truth is purely accidental.

I have been thinking about the book for some time, but as everything that follows is a little pinch of reality, and sometimes just a single event, tying them together into a book has proved to be extremely difficult.

I have my granddaughter Megan to thank for showing me how this could be done. Megan is never quiet. I had picked her up from school to run her home and part way her normal conversation (monologue actually) stopped for about five seconds. When it restarted, her first words were "Couldn't you tell I was choking on a sweet?" I had to tell her that I thought it had been unusual for her to be quiet for so long. And she replied that she had been quiet once before when she went to see The Lion King. *That was four years earlier!* How right she was, that would have been about the last time she was quiet! But it didn't matter, the connection had been made, my duck had been broken, it set me thinking that I could turn single events into sensible sized lumps of reading by using ridiculously tenuous connections, and it didn't matter if they were years apart! Thanks Meg!

As you read on you will find that some chapters have a little preamble which connects the events within them together, whilst others are single story. The chapters, therefore cannot be chronological and indeed, events within the chapters are not in any particular order, and this is principally because my mind is a shambles.

The inspiration for the book has been my family and friends who accidentally feature largely in it, and without whom I would not be surrounded by such daft folk, and would therefore have nothing to write about.

Thanks to:- My long suffering wife:- Jackie

My wonderful kids:- Emma, David, Pollyanne and Becky

All the assorted grandchildren, and the rest of my family and friends, most of whom now require a sincere apology from yours truly for exposing their weaker moments.

Contents

1
A Shower of Sh**

There are times when you know that you really shouldn't laugh about something, but the something in question keeps coming into your mind in a totally random sort of way, resulting in anything from a sneaky, wry smile to an uncontrollable short burst of air through the laughing gear (at least I think that it is random, but there may be semi-malicious sub-conscious forces at work as there sometimes are between couples who have been together for over thirty years). I need to explain.

The in laws, the Downs, had been having a spot of bother with the loo. The offending device was taking increasingly longer and longer to drain away, and being a resourceful and fairly close knit family we, that is, Jackie (my wife), and my two brothers in law, Stan and Neil with the help of yours truly decided to solve the problem once and for all and one fine sunny Saturday we decided on a three pronged attack on the drainage system.

Stan was in possession of a set of drain rods as a result of an astute purchase at some time in the misty past, and these had been lying in pristine condition, at the back of a pile of astute purchases in his garage, guarded by a tangle of cobwebs, just waiting for the perfect opportunity to be put into use.

Having scrambled over the astute purchases, Stan indicated from the back of the garage that the drain rods had been located. But instead of the sound of drain rods being dredged from the depths of the garage, there was utter silence. No movement , no speech, just silence.

From my leaning post on the twin tub I was on the point of becoming concerned and was about to make the appropriate enquiry as to whether everything was OK, when with a series of clatters and bangs, Stan emerged over the top of my head, like a shell from a gun, clearing it by several feet, and not stopping until he was half way down the garden. White as a sheet and with his eyes wide with fear he stood there in silence as disturbed bric-a-brac continued to settle back into place. "Flamin' 'eck, what's up?" I enquired.

"You should see the size of that bloody spider!" came the withered reply. "It must be three inches across!"

"A spider. You are kidding me! I thought there must be a Jap hiding out in yer jungle. I'll get them".

"I think there's only one!" shouted Stan from his safe area.

"I'm not getting the spider, I'm getting the drain rods" I replied.

I have to say, I claim to be 'not scared' of spiders, but this was a beast, a real masterpiece of genetic engineering. And the beast had been busy. There in the corner above the pile of drain rods, was a small frog, trussed up in a silk cocoon and hanging up, slowly rotating back and forth in the breeze dangling by a single silken strand, ready for lunch. I decided the best plan of action was to make a quick grab for the drain rods and make my exit quickly, whilst trying to look as I was not terrified of the eight legged garage monster.

Round at the In laws, Jackie's mum and dad Flo and Ben were inside making everyone a cup of tea. The manhole cover was already removed, revealing a slow trickle emerging from the pipe down from the loo. Neil was poking a stick as far up the pipe as it would go, without much success. There was a bend a couple of feet upstream from the manhole and it was becoming clear that whatever was blocking the pipe was above this point.

We unloaded the drain rods, a ladder, pick axe, garden spades, and set to work. Before long, the ladder was propped against the house wall and I was ascending and descending leaving assorted drain rods in the gutter above. Down below Jackie was in charge of my health and safety, ensuring the bottom of the ladder did not move from its prescribed position.

Under the ladder work began on removing paving slabs and earth to get down to the bend. I began connecting drain rods together and lowering the hooked end section by section until I started to feel some resistance. By twisting and lifting up and down I was managing to make steady progress into the sludge. Meanwhile below, earth was being removed and ancient pot sewage pipes started to appear.

My progress was beginning to falter, the last twenty minutes or so had produced nothing and I was beginning to think that this would be a long job. A shout from below rang out. "There's a root from the Honeysuckle found it's way through the joint in the pipe"

"Well I don't see it being that" I replied "but can you pull it out?" Stan immediately began pulling on the offending root. There was a crack as a small piece of the pipe broke away leaving Stan on his backside below. A homogenised mixture of freshly liquefied poo and urine came out of the new opening, with several feet of pressure head behind it, clearing the now prostrate Stan, just missing my boots, but shooting several feet above Jackie's head, before heading back down to earth, scoring a direct hit, and as the pressure began to drop, the evil smelling golden brown jet lowered it's trajectory, and completed the job.

Health and safety seemed suddenly to be less of a concern, as Jackie stepped back from the ladder, far too late to avoid the shower, and now utterly and completely covered from head to toe. The protestations, having started as a scream, continued "Eeeurgh, eeurgh, eeurgh."

"Eeurgh" we all thought.

There was crap everywhere, but by some strange twist of fate, no one apart from Jackie had been sprayed. By the time I got down from the ladder, Jackie was in the shower. I was thankful on this occasion that I had been too slow getting down from the ladder to have to give a supportive hug, or to kiss things better.

Further investigations into the blockage revealed a plug of Honeysuckle root the full diameter of the pipe and over a foot from end to end, it must have been filtering out what it wanted from the juice for months, but having got too greedy, managed to seal the whole thing off.

With a fresh supply of clothes for Jackie from home and having finished the job off with a new section of pipe, we headed for home. "Well", I said, "not a bad day, we have achieved two things."

"Two things?" was Jackie's questioning reply.

"Yep. Sorted your mum's loo and", (I became aware of the beginnings of a frown),"and given ourselves something to laugh at for the rest of our lives."

"You're right," she said, "It was funny wasn't it?". 'Top lass' I thought.

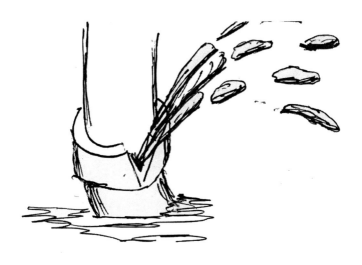

2

The Starfish and the Whale

It is really great to have friends. We tend to have just a few close friends, and dozens of people of the sort that you would stop in the street and pass a couple of minutes with, just to catch up on how they are. Otley is that sort of a place. Familiar faces everywhere. We count the O'Deigh's, Tim and Dawn, as our closest friends, I suppose that it was inevitable that we would become friends, Tim and I were in the same year at Weston Lane School up to being 11, and he just lived around the corner. Living on the Estate in those days was a special thing. There were hundreds of kids all the same age or with just a few years between us, none of us realised how bad things must have been just a few short years earlier when almost the whole world was at war and our parents were all players in the horror.

The years passed and by the mid 70's our generation had for the large part gone our separate ways. Jackie had lived on the next street when she was younger, and when we started 'going out' in the late 60's she still lived on the north side of the river but not on the Weston Estate. Tim had joined the Navy, but when he left he also came back home to Otley. Dawn we jokingly describe as an outsider, she hails from Burley in Wharfedale, just across the river Wharfe, it can't be more than a mile from Weston Estate, but to get there is a four mile trip through the centre of town to avoid finishing up floating down the Humber past Hull.

Once you have lived somewhere with a community spirit like Otley you get drawn back to your roots, and having lived away for just a few short years, there we were, a generation later, back on the Estate. Our kids, Emma, David, Pollyanne and Becky were similar ages to the O'Deigh's kids, Ben, Eve, April and Holly and often played together. No real surprise then that we became good friends and amongst other things, now the kids have grown up and left home, we go on holiday together. Now you should know that we are all a bit on the large size, all be it to varying degrees.

We are not the sort of people to go and sit on the same beach or by a pool every day, doing nothing, or stand in a bar all night. We like our holidays to be varied and interesting, sometimes with unexpected results.

A friend of ours had rented us a cottage in North Wales, one of our favourite places, and the four of us set forth in the trusty Astra Estate. We had a scorching week, so the fact that we spent the occasional hour messing about on the beach was unusual but not surprising. Abersoch is a lovely place. Lots of people messing about in boats, or just enjoying the warm (relatively) gulf stream water. We had decided to avail ourselves of a rubber dinghy, a nice 'two man' blue and yellow effort with a rope around the side.

To say millpond would be no exaggeration, a few miles away at Hells Mouth the prevailing wind makes sure that the breakers are large enough to make it worth getting out the surfboards, but here, at the southern end of Abersoch beach, the sea would often come in and go out without breaking a single wave. After great personal effort inflating the beast which made me wish that we had purchased the smaller unit and taken our boating pleasure on an individual basis, the dinghy was launched and I was installed, with oars in the hoops, ready to take out my passenger.

You would think that someone who was ex-navy would have fared a little better than Tim actually managed. As he lifted his leg to get in a wave caught the dinghy, and the rope created a loop around his foot. There was fear on his face as the second wave caught the dinghy and the rope dragged at his leg, removing fifty percent of his support. His position quickly changed from vertical to horizontal, there he was, laid out like a starfish on his back in six inches of seawater. The third and fourth waves broke over the unfortunate Tim, who was still attached by one foot to the side of the dinghy. There was a splutter. Then having expelled the seawater, and in finest profane Yorkshire dialect, asked if I was "Trying to bloody well drown him". A fifth wave shut him up, good job too, there were children on the beach!

There was more floundering and Tim managed to extricate his foot from its mobile moorings, and scramble to his feet to find Dawn and Jackie literally crying with laughter at his starfish impression. "I'm off to the loo" he grunted. On his return and finding that the hilarity had not abated, he declined the invitation to "have a go in the dinghy" and chose to sunbathe, thinking it was a safer option than venturing out into the dangerous waters of the bay. This turned out to be the more dangerous choice of the two as Tim managed to get the worst case of sunburnt feet that I have ever seen, come to think of it, the only case of sunburnt feet I have ever seen.

The following day was another scorcher, we drove up to Harlech to have a look around the castle, and then had an ice cream in the village. We found our way down on to the beach and sat watching the world go by. Dawn got herself settled down reading a book but soon started to doze. We decided that she looked far too comfortable, and being time to move on, we, that is Tim and I, decided to dig a ditch at either side of her. Purely for experimental purposes of course! The soft windblown sand that forms Harlech beach started to slide away, and slowly but surely, Dawn started to sink.

The sinking had the desired effect of waking Tim's delicate little Yorkshire flower, who uttered a string of profanities that, quite frankly, we expected! Dawn aimed her reading book accurately at Tim's ear. "Ow!" "We're ready to go. Do you want a hand up?"

The profanity continued: "Bugger off prat, I'll get up meself".

We collected our beach mats and the lemonade bottle. Meanwhile Dawn rolled first one way and then the other, then back again trying to extricate herself from the shallow pit. Tim was by now half way back to the car park, I don't know if this was due to embarrassment or a malicious sense of humour or whether he was simply obeying the instruction to "bugger off". Dawn continued to do an impression of a beached whale until she made enough sideways progress to grab a handy fence post which she used to help herself up. "Prat. Tim! Tim! Ruddy prat." Looking like a meatloaf freshly rolled in flour, Dawn set off across the sand intent on using the reading book on Tim's hearing equipment again.

Tim was back at the car by now. Jackie and I were back seconds later. We were quickly installed in the car, three of us sniggering at the recent sight of this large lady rolling about on the beach, trying to get purchase on something to help herself up. Dawn dusted herself down and looked less than chuffed.

"Prats" she said.

3
Benllech and Ballachbeama

I am absolutely convinced that people can have premonitions about things which are about to happen, although this is completely foreign to my logical scientific mind, and I have to say that I would not believe other than the fact that on more than one occasion I have had feelings and dreams about things which have then proceeded to happen within a couple of days. I am also convinced that what will happen cannot be changed. There may be millions of possibilities but there is only one path for the future.

When we were teenagers we had planned a family camping holiday but I had had bad feelings about the holiday beforehand. The day came and we all set off, heading for Anglesey, Mum and Dad in our family car, my Auntie, Uncle and cousin in their car and Jackie and myself on the trusty Lambretta. To be honest we had a good journey down and we started to have an excellent camping holiday in the tiny resort of Benllech.

Most of Benllech is up away from the sea, the main road choosing to ignore the pleasant little bay which is reached by a minor road from the crossroads, and which winds its way down the hill and levels out just a few feet above high water level below grassy mud cliffs about the height of a couple of houses. It really is a pleasant walk along the seafront road to the café where there is a ramp down to the beach. The beach is rarely fully covered but at high tide the sea breaks over the rocks and hits the sea wall at the bottom of the hill down from the crossroads, often with spectacular results.

Sunday morning was warm and the sky was clear. Jackie and I were walking down to the café. A group of elegantly attired ladies had their deck chairs perched on top of the grassy cliffs, sunning themselves and watching the world go by. The road was very wet when we got to the bottom of the hill, so we had an idea that we might get a bit of a soaking, but being full of teenage bravado we decided to stick with the path along the seaward side of the road rather than cross over to the cliff where there was no path.

Before we had run the gauntlet of the spray, a huge wave broke against the sea wall, instead of getting a soaking, the wave created a column of water a few yards in front of us. It is incomprehensible how much power went into creating the huge water column, the volume was immense and the height was staggering. As gravity took over its tremendous force removed some of the cliff top sunbathers from their deckchairs, and thoroughly soaked the rest. One of the group got to her feet and screamed, the rest, I presume, were too stunned by this unexpected soaking to do anything. "Clearly sinners" I said as we began to run towards the café.

From then the holiday took a bit of a downward turn. The gear cable went on the Lambretta, but being resourceful, we managed to figure a way of changing gear by utilising a ring spanner bolted to the top of the gear change mechanism in order to get to Caernarfon, this involved me shouting "up" or "down" to Jackie at the appropriate moment. Jackie would then move the end of the spanner backwards or forwards to give the desired gear change. The problem was quickly sorted and we made our way back to Anglesey using a more conventional, but less fun, method to find our way around the gearbox.

The following day my uncle had a bump in the car, this left the entire front of his Morris 1100 several inches out of line with the rest of the vehicle. We decided to finish the holiday early, but before we had even got off the island, the Lambretta developed a front wheel puncture at 50mph. This is a very unpleasant experience. When you have a front wheel puncture in a car you lose a great deal of control. On two wheels you really don't know what is going to happen next. With the bike banked over to go round the sweeping right hand bend we were negotiating, we were still going straight on, that is until we hit the kerb. Luckily for us there were no stone walls of other obstructions where we came adrift, otherwise things could have been far worse. As it turned out someone had seen our demise and called for an ambulance, which arrived promptly and sped Jackie off to Bangor Hospital. I changed the wheel and followed on, a few stitches and jabs later and we were on our way, only slightly worse for the experience.

Another occasion where I had had a vivid premonition about a place was when the O'Deigh's, Tim and Dawn along with Jackie and myself went to County Kerry on holiday. The dream was very clear and it occurred about three times in the week before we went. In the dream we were travelling through an empty landscape without fences, and heading towards a cliff face. Even when we got close to the cliff face, there did not appear to be a way through. I could not have imagined how closely my dream would match the centre of County Kerry and the approach to the Ballachbeama pass.

County Kerry is a wonderful place. If you are looking for stunning scenery, here it is. If you are prepared to be amazed by absolute desolation then it can also be found. It is a long way from Dublin and by the time we got to Killorglin we had realised that not all Irish roads were, let us say, smooth running. But we are never phased by these things. The trusty Astra generally copes.

We were staying in a static caravan in a medium sized site a few miles north of Killorglin. The view of the mountains from the caravan window was great but the site did hold the odd surprise. By far means the oddest were the couple who ran the site. They lived in one of the static caravans, but the layout was somewhat customised. They had double doors straight into the living room, where there was a double bed where they spent their lives watching the TV set!

When we ran out of gas we turned up and knocked on the door, and we were asked if we knew how to connect a new bottle up. Then we were given instruction as to where to collect the bottle from. It was apparently OK to leave the empty one by the caravan as he would collect it later. "Thanks" we thought, don't overdo it.

Still, Killorglin was nice enough and there was occasional entertainment in the pubs of a musical kind, and most nights the pubs would remain open until the last man fell over. The Irish pub singer however did turn out to be one of the few Norwegians who can hold a note.

Saturday was interesting. A group of locals came in a little worse for wear, one on the point of collapse. One of the group brought him across to where we were sitting and asked if he could sit him on the spare seat at our table before he fell over. We obliged. Once parked, his head sank to the table. After a short while it became clear that we were being observed by our new friend, from his vantage point in the middle of several glasses of beer. "You'll not be Irish then?" Came the slurred statement from our observer. ---- We weren't.---- We explained that we were English, from Yorkshire. "Oh", he said in a moment of lucidity, "Do you know, I worked there once." ---- We didn't know of course.

Our table guest was soon fast asleep, starting off with his arms cushioning his head on the table, but slowly sinking, bit by bit until his head was in Jackie's lap, and there he lay, snoring loudly. In his next moment of clarity he opened his eyes, looked up at Jackie and said "Cookridge". This was followed another ten minutes coma!

After he had come round a bit and returned his

head to a more suitable position we explained that we all lived within five miles of Cookridge and that Jackie and I had a daughter who lived there. Now we had a new friend. He summoned his brother over, who apologised for the state of his sibling. We said he was no bother at all. The second brother was informed that we all lived near Cookridge. Suddenly we were the finest English people the brothers had met and we had two new friends.

On the Monday we went to explore Killarney. The town itself is nice but unremarkable, but hidden behind a high stone wall and down a long drive is the lakeside Ross Castle, you can ride from the centre of Killarney down to this wonderful spot in a Hansom Cab, there are dozens of them running a shuttle service up and down. Having looked around and had a pleasant picnic, our attention was drawn to boats coming and going, taking people out into the lake. We enquired and one of the trips available was a ride out to Inishfallen Abbey, a ruin on an island in the lake. The boatman explained that one of the options was to be dropped off on the island by one boat, and picked up by the next, giving about three quarters of an hour to explore the island and the abbey.

We decided to go and explore. Once we got out into the lake I noticed a striking resemblance between our pilot and the boat owner in the Jaws film, the one who drove his boat flat out until the engine blew up. He even wore the same hat! I signalled silently to Tim and made a shark sign with my hand and pointed at my lower jaw. He looked puzzled but when I pointed with a hidden finger at our guide he looked at me with a look of mock fear. How I kept a straight face I do not know. We were duly dropped off on the island and bade our pilot "Goodbye" and "take it steady" As he disappeared out of sight we did a risk analysis of crossing the lake and decided that the population density of the local great white shark was sparse enough not to worry about the pilot and his boat being eaten before he had a chance to collect us from the island.

The following day we had decided to follow an interesting looking route on the map through a place called Glencar and over the mountains at Ballachbeama. Beyond Glencar the country opens out and there is a vast open plain with nothing for miles. No houses, no fences, no cattle, no sheep, just grass! It amused us somewhat that in typical Irish fashion, someone had chosen to allow a sign to be placed several miles along this road into the wilderness, announcing that this was a "**COMMUNITY ALERT AREA**". Someone had obviously been testing how alert the local community were by blasting the sign several times with a shotgun.

We crossed a hump back bridge and headed towards the pass. After a short while it became clear that something was badly wrong. A series of loud bangs from the back of the car gave us no option but to stop immediately. Laid underneath the rear end of the ailing Astra I quickly determined that one of the rear dampers had broken free of its lower mounting leaving just a short piece of thread sticking out. Resourcefully, having relocated the remains of the damper in the suspension arm, I managed to jam a nut on to the bottom of the stump of the thread, but with the rubber bush gone, I was not holding out too much hope. We headed for the vertical cliff face that I had seen in my dream. The road took a sharp left and disappeared behind a rock revealing a steep narrow passage between two sections of the cliff.

The spectacularly uneven road comprised tarmac laid on top of the rocks and my wonderful repair lasted about two miles. We had no option but to pull in and call for assistance. Thank goodness for mobile phones. It took some time to explain where we were to the control centre up in Scotland but we finally got the message across. "Where's the nearest town?"

"I think it's Kenmare" I replied.

"Aha! Ballachbeama" the man said, followed by a short silence. "Heck! basically you are up a mountain miles from anywhere, there's no garage in Kenmare, we'll have to send someone from Killarney, but we won't be able to get there in an hour"

Never mind, we thought, It's a nice day, we can have a picnic, play cards, sit and admire the view. Danny rang

"I'm coming to get yuz. Where are yuh?" I explained again. "Ah, Blageema it is. Sure, that's right." came the knowledgeable reply "I think I know where that is" We were not filled with confidence. We admired the view for an hour and a half. Three cyclists came down the hill and disappeared into the distance. We went back to admiring the view. One by one we hid behind the wall to pee. I'm not sure who we were hiding from. We played cards, we played I spy [nothing to spy], and then we admired the view. Another hour and a half later, a very nice man turned up with his rescue truck. With the window wound down, he shouted "Is there anywhere to torn round?"

"There's a viewpoint at the top of the pass, you should be able to turn round there."

Danny eyed the road up. "Nope, *NOT* going up thor." Danny replied. Considering the width and ridiculous incline of the road, Danny did a fine 15 point turn to point the truck in the right direction. "There's four of yuz", Danny stated the obvious, "trucks only got two seats."

"Two seats?" we questioned.

"That's right!" said Danny. Our hearts sank. Danny suggested a Taxi. Tim and I swivelled round a full circle in each direction before facing Danny with our mouths open. I'm not sure if it was the thought of spending another two or three hours on this desolate mountain road, or the thought of having to pay a taxi to do a sixty mile round trip to Killarney that left us stood there catching flies. "Or", Danny continued, "yous two could sneak into the car while I'm not looking".

"What? Up there?" we questioned.

"That's right!" said Danny.

We leapt at the chance without really thinking things through. Danny strapped the car down and we set off on a white knuckle ride of epic proportions. We made our way down to the bottom of the pass with the truck bouncing about and swaying from side to side. The car was perched on top amplifying the motion. It probably didn't help that one of the dampers was dangling in space and about as much use as a chocolate fireman. Jackie and Dawn kept looking round to see if the car was still there. After several miles, to the relief of Tim and I, we found ourselves on a main road. The relief lasted about four miles. Danny stopped the truck and tightened the straps.

"You're tightening the straps eh?" I said questioningly.

"That's right" said Danny and climbed back in the cab without further explanation. We soon found out why. We were on a main road, but a very old Irish road in *serious* need of re-laying.

The road followed a cliff with a lake at the bottom, probably a thousand feet below. Tim was white. Jackie and Dawn looked back at us with mouths wide open. I put my seat belt on. Tim said "if we go you will need a bloody parachute not a seat belt".

"That's right" I thought. The road bounced on, somehow we didn't take much notice of the spectacular 'Ladies View', by now we had had all the viewpoints we could take in.

As the road wound down to Killarney we started to feel a little more secure, the smell of involuntary farts was beginning to clear, and Jackie and Dawn seemed to be able to raise a smile. We ground to a halt for roadworks. We waved and smiled weakly at the man on a huge road roller who was amazed to be eye to eye with two terrified idiots in a bouncing Astra on the back of a car transporter. The man with the stop-go board laughed out loud and lost his concentration and turned his board to 'go' before we got past. We left the resulting chaos in our wake as we travelled further down the hill. We sank as low as we could while we went through the streets of Killarney.

At the garage the car was lowered off the back of the truck and Danny said in mock surprise as we got out. "Ah now what were yous two doing in there?"

"Sh**ting ourselves", I replied

"That's right!" said Danny.

4
Hair

I had the unfortunate experience of being robbed in our local Netto store. My pocket was expertly picked, and I never felt a thing until it was too late. I rarely have money in any quantity in my pocket, but this being the week before Christmas, I had drawn £100 for bits and pieces. I was looking at the shelves when a woman, a real double bagger*, who was stood next to me picked a toy up from the shelf and stated to fiddle with it. "Can you get this working?" she asked in a thick accent. Foolishly, I obliged, unaware that my wallet had already been removed from my pocket and the cash was being removed by an accomplice standing behind me. The woman walked off and as I moved away from the shelf, my now empty wallet (which is attached by a chain) hit me on the knee.

I raised the alarm immediately, but the woman and the pickpocket were nowhere in sight. Cleverly there was a third person involved who collected the money from the pickpocket. How do I know so much detail? Because it all happened immediately under a CCTV camera which gave crystal clear pictures of the whole thing!

Watching the playback in the managers office it struck me how thin I was getting on top, then it struck me how vain it was that I could ignore the fact that I had been robbed for long enough to think about the fact that I was starting to get a hole in my hairzone layer.

Hair is a funny thing. It starts to lose it's sense of direction when you are about thirteen, and as you get older it is the first part of the body to get senile. It forgets what colour it should be and mine has now got to the stage where it has forgotten to grow on the top of my head, so I am expecting that once this crop has worn out that there won't be any more. On the other hand, it seems to grow in copious quantities from my nose, ears, and chin. Also, if it were not for regular trimming, my eyebrows would make Dennis Healey look like an alopecia sufferer.

Tim is to say the least, follically challenged and has been since his twenties. To give him his due, he has never been tempted to resort to the comb over to cover the fact that his pride and joy has long gone. We do joke about it when he says he needs a haircut. "which one?" and "Get the magnifying glass, I'll do it " are just typical. Tim's smooth hairless cranium has also given rise to the name we give our pub quiz team, 'Aaron no Hair'.

Not all bald men are as accepting of their fate. I remember we used to get regular visits from a machinery supplier. He had an awful wig. It was ginger to match his colouring, but that must have been some time before because the gentleman's own remains of hair were turning from grey to white, giving a sort of tinted fringe effect around the neck. The effect was spectacularly bad, and your eyes were drawn to it, making it utterly impossible to make eye contact with the guy.

We are in the habit of occasionally going to the Carnival at Weston Super Mare. This event occurs in early November, it really is a stunning display, with well over a hundred illuminated, mechanically animated floats, involving several million light bulbs.

You would think that a particularly stunning, prize winning float, would be what we remember most about the Carnival, but when we think back there is only one particular thing that stands out. Spectacular it was, but not a light in site.

Carnival floats do not always move at the same speed, and in particular, in this carnival, huge floats, towing massive generator sets are expected to negotiate sharp bends. No surprise that there are often large gaps in the parade. In one of these gaps, a couple crossed the road towards us. She was a twenty something blonde, I think. And you would expect that we would notice her as opposed to her partner, as red blooded males have a tendency to do. Did we heck!

The worst comb over in the world, *ever* was coming towards us.

It comprised several strands of hair carefully combed from the back of the neck. This was carefully formed into a strip of hair about two inches in width, leaving a bald strip either side above the ears. There had obviously been some time spent on this, as this narrow section of hair had been combed forward and lacquered down in a series of perfectly straight lines to the front of the shiny pink dome. This work of minimalist hair art had then been carefully trimmed to form a kind of fringe.

As the couple walked through the gap in the barriers between Tim and I standing at the side of the road we turned spellbound, and our faces came to a point where each could see the expression on the other. "Don't laugh yet" I thought "-you will set me off". We looked away but only to see Jackie and Dawn who were stood open mouthed in disbelief. Super-*Mare*-man was by now already legend.

I hope no one thought that we were laughing hysterically at the carnival floats! Can anyone remember what the theme of the carnival was that year?

* A double bagger is someone who should not be allowed out without a bag over their heads for fear of scaring folk. Two bags for safety purposes!

5
Maggots and Dishwater

What a wonderful place the Yorkshire Dales is, and from where we were brought up , in Otley , the area is so accessible. As kids we used to walk up to Weston woods or climb on our bikes and explore a bit further afield. One Easter when I was about 14 my cousin, Sparrer Jackson,(N.B. Jackson-> Jackdaw ->Sparrer) and I decided to go camping. We persuaded my uncle to load our gear up in his Jowett van and drop us off in a camping field at Appletreewick. We thought that it would be fun to take in a bit of fishing and walking. We selected a pitch and had no trouble at all putting up our ancient ridge tent in glorious spring sunshine, although thinking back we might have picked a better layout for things inside the tent.

By now it was lunchtime and we grabbed a sandwich and decided to go for a walk. We both donned a trilby hat, mine had a green feather, and set off for Barden Tower, a few miles down the valley. After a fun two or three minutes exploring the nettles that had taken residence in this ancient keep, we decided to head back. The fickle dales weather was about to spring a few surprises. The wind got up. The temperature plummeted. The skies opened and threw a torrent of almost horizontal rain and sleet at us. The green feather was wrecked, and so was the trilby.

Never mind we thought, we can get a warm drink when we get back, and dry out in the tent. We noticed a group of teenage lads had planted their tents on the islands in the middle of the River Wharfe, and felt slightly jealous that we had not thought of that. We were soon back in the tent. It seems that our first mistake had been to leave various items of food open such as bread and biscuits, our second mistake was to hang the bag of maggots on a slightly less than secure hook, our third mistake was that the said insecure hook was directly above our box of food. The wind had shaken the tent enough to remove the bag from its hanging place and now the maggots were feasting on everything that was not in a tin.

The ancient canvas of our rickety tent was a little less than waterproof and we had to walk about a mile to the village to purchase a box of dry matches. We slept fully clothed in damp sleeping bags that night. Unpleasant. Some time around midnight the rotten canvas of my camp bed, probably a wartime leftover, decided to rip from end to end leaving me perched atop the joints of the three wooden legs. The bed was quickly ejected from the tent but the floor was very cold and the thought of maggots running around on it kept me awake for an age.

Having nicely dropped off, I was awakened in the early hours by a blasphemous uttering from the other side of the tent. When I opened my eyes it was obvious something was seriously wrong. The tent was about three inches from my face! Sparrer, being still on a camp bed, was higher up than me was supporting the structure with his laid out body. We scrambled along to the 'door' to find that there had been about six inches of snow during the night. There was abundant foul language, and we decided that our only option was to get up and sort out the problem.

As it got lighter we realised that the lads camping on the islands were going to be in serious trouble. The river was now at a level where you would not be able to wade across if, and lapping at the banks of the islands. Before long the Mountain Rescue service arrived in a Land Rover, and we were witnesses to a spectacular rope rescue across the raging Wharfe. It was the high spot of our holiday.

Many years later our little holiday club (Tim, Dawn, Jackie and I) felt that we were getting too large on an individual basis and we decided that we should try to reduce our excess lard problem by having a walking holiday in the dales. Rather than setting off and aiming for somewhere, we did a series of pre-planned walks at various points in the Yorkshire dales. Some but not all involved stopping at some pub for lunch. This gave us the chance to explore a large and varied area of the Yorkshire dales in one week.

One particular walk saw us hiking through a series of extremely small fields enclosed with stone walls. Some of the walls were as close as 10 yards apart (honest!). This meant that there were quite a few 'stiles'. Now whether the walls had moved since the stiles were put in I am not sure, or more likely the stiles may just have been intended to be sheep proof, bearing in mind that the sheep could well have been underfed, unless they were penned individually in the tiny fields. Whatever reason, there was certainly a design flaw which would be a problem for anyone over eight stones. The stiles consisted of very narrow gaps in the walls bordered by a pair of full height vertical stones. Some of the stiles were narrower than my walking boots, which did not make for a graceful transfer from one field to the next. My problem was nothing compared to Dawn's. She did not have a boot problem, as her feet are very small, but her posterior is somewhat larger and closer to the ground than mine and she had to arrange to shoehorn one buttock at a time. With some hilarity we had to rescue her from one stile where she was perched with both feet well clear of the ground. We wished we had videoed the incident to make a few bob.

Having fought valiantly to make progress for some time we decided to stop for a brew. Now, Dawn is renowned for taking her tea very weak indeed, she always asks for the teabag to be left out when she orders tea in a restaurant, so the bag can be given a brief dip in order to produce an insipid brew that none of the rest of us would thank you for.

Jackie and I sat down and poured tea from our flask. Tim started to do the same and complained as the liquid entered the cups that Dawn had catered for her taste in tea and not given a thought to anyone who would want a decent brew. Tim took a large swig and quickly sprayed the large swig across the field. Once the offending liquid was ejected, and the foul language had died down to an intelligible level, Tim shouted, "Dishwater urgh! Urgh! I've drunk mucky 'orrible dish-bloody-water! Dawn! I thought you made the tea."

"No" came the reply "you made the tea."

"I think you will find that no one made the flippin' tea", I interjected.

It seemed like we had all had enough of our drinks, so we headed for the Green Dragon pub. We made excellent progress in relative silence, apart from Tim mumbling, "I've carried bloody dishwater all this bloody way" and "I've drunk mucky 'orrible dishwater" every few yards and of course the odd burst of uncontrollable laughter from the rest of us. It obviously took several pints to wash the taste away, good job I was driving! And I still wonder what the barman thought when Tim kept repeating the words, "Dishwater , bloody dishwater" as he downed his beer.

6
Phut, Phut

When we were teenagers we used to love messing about with motorbikes and scooters, but most of all Lambrettas.

My cousin John, or should I say his dad, my uncle John, had a garage on the land at the back of his house. Most of the houses around the block had a garage at the back, all surrounding a bit of an open gravel clearing, and we quite often used to mess about around here, generally tinkering or rebuilding something. We were often out there in all weathers or at all times of day.

The garage next to John's was derelict. It had belonged to a neighbour, Mr Lawton, who had reversed the car out of the garage one day with a misted up rear window. Instead of cleaning the window, he decided to open the drivers door to look behind. The door caught on the upright holding the front of the garage up, and once this support had been removed, the garage belly flopped on to the car in spectacular style and both garage and car were complete and utter wrecks.

I seem to remember it took him a while to emerge from the car, to the point where our suppressed hilarity was becoming concern, whether the time taken was through shock or embarrassment we will never know. But after the dust had settled, emerge he did, unscathed. As he walked away from this scene of utter devastation in the direction of the bus stop, carrying his lunch bag, his only words were "Bugger!.... Bugger!"

Now, we had had an old Lambretta engine in the corner of the garage for some time and it had become covered in cobwebs. We had forgotten where it had come from, and we really did not hold out much hope for it working. However, we decided we would assemble it and test it. We had managed to get an old Lambretta frame, and we decided that since there was no kick start, we would have to put the old engine together with the frame and bounce it off.

To be perfectly honest, in our enthusiasm, we did cut a few corners. There was, for example, no front brake. Oh, and no back brake! There was no seat. The little lever that brings the fuel tap out to an accessible point, we didn't bother with. There was no working ignition lock, and no cut out button! We chose not to bother with the gear change, or the clutch although I do remember some discussion around the fact of whether the engine was in first or second gear. We did connect up the exhaust pipe and pushed a silencer box on to it, without tightening the clamp of course. We didn't bother with an air filter. The only control was the throttle.

None of this really mattered as the rusty old thing was never going to start, or if it did we were only going to fire it up and do a lap of the garage site in Speedway style and then stop.

The plan was for yours truly to sit on the ugly beast while John and Sparrer ran, holding the back wheel off the ground, dropping it at an appropriate time. I expect most people have by now spotted a *slight* flaw in the plan, and I think it must have been enthusiasm that was the reason that I hadn't. I was about to get a rude awakening.

Fuelled up and ready for the little test. We were proud of the 'thing'. My two cousins ran and dropped the back wheel. 'Phut' To our astonishment the engine fired. Enthusiastically I opened the throttle. Phut…….. phut……phut. Not quite one firing of the engine per lamppost but clearly this was not first gear. Or second. And I was rapidly running out of garage site. I released the throttle. Phut….phut…phut..phut.

The engine was labouring but there was no doubt about it, it was getting faster, even with the throttle shut. We hadn't adjusted the cable! To make matters worse it was becoming clear which gear I was in: fourth! I was already out of the garage site and down the back road. Phut.phut.phut. Now it started to dawn on me that I had no method of stopping or even slowing down our marvellous machine.

I hurtled out of the end of the back road, on to on of the estate's minor roads. Phut phutphutputput. Out I shot on to Meagill Rise, luckily for me there was nothing coming in either direction because by now my speed was not conducive to taking sharp left handers. I started to think quickly, if I could find the right wire, I could short out the ignition and stop the thing. All the wires that should go to the ignition switch were there and I started to fiddle. Nothing worked. I have to say that working out what was what while careering down the road out of control past rows of parked cars is taking multi tasking just a shade too far. My trusty steed continued. Putputpupupupup.

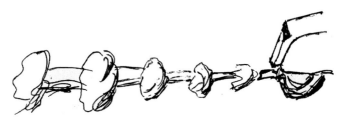

I banked the 'thing' over as I ran out of road at the end of Meagill Rise, and I was on Weston Drive. I decided to try something else. I leant over to the left at a crazy angle and put my hand over the carburettor inlet. Grrrrrrrrrrrrrr r r r r. The engine started to die. But the suction was too much and I had to remove my hand before the 'thing' gave me a giant blood blister. Phut….phut…phut..phut.phut. The damned thing was off again. I started to think about where I could ditch it, or maybe if there was no one on the green, I could ride round and round the football pitch until I ran out of fuel, but that could take hours.

As I passed the parade of shops, I had a plan to remove the plug cap from the spark plug. Once again leant the bike over at a crazy angle, this time to the right, and grabbed the plug cap. **Don't EVER do this**. Not only was I hurtling down the road, out of control, leaning over at a crazy angle, but I now had 40000 volts passing through me in a series of jolting pulses. For a moment it looked as though I was a cyclist furiously pedalling uphill with my backside elevated from the seat and wobbling up and down. Once I had extricated my hand from this electrical vice, which I did without managing to remove the plug cap, I came to the conclusion that crashing was my only option. I needed to arrange a soft landing and I knew where there was a bit of open land with bushes, and I hoped that they weren't hawthorn. I bounced up off the road. The silencer came off as I hit the kerb at breakneck speed, and as I reached the bush, I deliberately dropped the 'thing', which embedded itself in the bush and finally stalled.

"That got you, you ***bastard***" I said as I got to my feet, none the worse apart from a few scratches. An old lady waiting for a bus looked at me open mouthed. I picked up the silencer and pushed the deathtrap back to the garage site.

"It goes then" said John, as I returned. "It doesn't f**kin well stop though" I growled.

7
Fickle Weather

British weather is notoriously fickle, I say British as opposed to English, because I have no desire to upset those from Scotland or Wales who will state confidently that their weather is fickler than English weather, and I have to say that in my experience, the weather in those places can vary between lovely and truly awful, and it has a malicious streak!

Some time ago, when our four children, Emma, David, Pollyanne and Becky, were small we went on a camping holiday to Tenby, we had heard that the weather was pleasant and the sea was warm, being directly in the gulf stream.

We duly installed our tent at the bottom of the long camping field, set all the gear out, and as is our usual way, wasted no time at all in starting to explore the area, and Tenby was our primary destination.

The first few days were pleasant enough, we were camped too far out of town to walk, so we drove in and parked, the car park attendant was a pleasant, talkative sort of bloke who fancied himself as a weather forecaster. Each day as we left the car park, he would say "there's bad weather coming you know"

We did have the odd shower, but it didn't stop the fun. The kids played on the beach, or ran around the camp site doing kid things. We also got time to go for the odd outing elsewhere. One of these was a Mediaeval Fayre, a thoroughly enjoyable day out, with jousting demonstrations, and hundreds of other themed stalls. Oh, and a fire engine, which was taking children up in the cherry picker.

As we came away having thoroughly enjoyed the outing, our David, who was about five at the time, came out with the wonderful line, "Well, I don't think that that was very mad. Or evil." [he had thought that we were going to a mad and evil fayre] Who knows what he was expecting!

The weather started to go downhill, Wednesday night was awful and we dug tiny trenches around the tent to take the worst excesses of the surface water away. On the Thursday, the rain was so bad that we decided to entertain ourselves in the swimming baths in order to stay dry. We had to wade across the car park in our wellies! When we got back to the tent, it was clear that we were not going to spend another night there as tapping the groundsheet of the bedrooms caused a ripple effect to travel outwards across the floor from the point of impact. We were camping in a giant puddle!

We decided there and then to pack up and go. Now we discovered that there had been a flaw in our plan when we cut the trenches, all our equipment, the tent, the car, us and the kids were plastered in mud. Soon everything was put away in the trailer, or the back of the car and we set off to go up the field.

No we didn't. The wheels went round and we made no progress whatsoever up the hill. Some people came across and helped us get moving, but now we were going across the field, not up. Luckily the field was by now almost abandoned which allowed me to make progress in a series of giant 'S' shaped loops, each one long enough to give us enough inertia to get to the next level. We must have travelled several miles up that field. When we got to the top we bundled all the kids out of the car, and into the showers. We had a complete set of dry, mud free clothing for all of us.

The drive home was done in one stint, stopping briefly near Derby and arriving home in the early hours having driven through what resembled a riverbed all the way. Now *that* is typical British summer weather.

Now I should explain that this was the only occasion where we cut a camping holiday short and we braved some rotten stuff in our time and never gave up. On one occasion we were camping near Rhyl, the weather was pleasant enough but unknown to us it was not going to last.

We had driven down into Rhyl in our blue Hillman Hunter the day before and had an awful half hour where we lost track of our Emma. Somehow we had got separated as we looked in the various gift shops. Now this is a horrible feeling, your own terror is mixed with the thoughts of what could be going through your child's mind, lost in a place that they have never seen before, heaving with traffic and people. To give Emma her due, at four years old she was resourceful enough to ask people if they had seen a Blue *Human* Hunter parked anywhere as it was her mum and dads.

As she came through the crowd towards us the relief was overwhelming, a couple had stayed with her until she found us, I don't think we ever thanked them properly, and I still feel guilty about that. It was probably a half hour she was missing, but it felt like an age.

On a lighter note, Rhyl at holiday times is full of Liverpuddlians. There is something special about the Liverpool accent that sets it apart, and there is something about the cheek of teenage Liverpuddlian lads out on the pull that sets them apart. Two such lads were in front of us walking down the street, obviously eyeing up the two girls walking in front of them. Now what happened next I am not recommending as a pick up line, because apart from absolutely guaranteeing a reaction, I don't think that it has any other plus points, and in any case it only works in a Liverpool accent.

Loudly, so that the girls could not fail to hear and in finest Liverpuddlian, one of the lads shouted "Looch at the posteeerior on thach!" The girls turned, looked, said nothing and continued on their way, posteriors swaying, lads following, we never found out how much success the lads had. Or indeed whether they survived.

That night the radio announced that there was to be a storm and gale force winds, and there were one or two people packed up there and then and left the camp site. The site was still very busy dozens of tents of all sizes and styles about. I decided to take heed of the warning and fix diagonals, using spare guy ropes to the internal tube work of our battered old frame tent, fixing the bottom of them to the ground with the largest tent pegs we could muster. Well fixed down, it did feel much sturdier. Having settled down for the night, we became aware of the storm hitting. We all slept surprisingly soundly, but on a couple of occasions we were woken by car lights coming on and some commotion. However, I really was not prepared for the scene the following morning.

Sticking my head out of the tent in the morning was a shock. There was rubbish everywhere, dustbins were blown over, here and there was abandoned camping equipment. In the tree nearby was a tent. And looking round, apart from ours, the one in the tree was the only tent on the site, not one other tent had survived the wind. Somehow it felt good, I did feel a little sorry for the other campers, but what the heck we were superior! We beat the weather! - Sorry campers!

8
The Bus

For most of the nineteen nineties we were the proud owners of a Volkswagen Minibus, not the tidiest example of the model around, but quite reliable and great fun. It was painted in a rather fetching wave design, and looked for all the world as though it belonged to a crowd of surfing fanatics. It was fitted with bench seats and had sturdy roof bars, and it meant that if we went on a long journey to a holiday destination we could pile all the gear up in the middle of the van so that the kids could not fight one another, a perfect packing up job meant that they could not even see each other to argue. Bliss.

I did do quite a lot of home maintenance on the van over the years, and in return it gave us good service. On one occasion I had decided to renew the doughnut coupling on the steering column. Jackie was in the van, holding the steering wheel, and I was underneath undoing the doughnut bolts. One of these came undone suddenly and I managed to hit myself in the head with the spanner, a ruddy great clobber of a hit as it happens. Immediately I felt blood running down the side of my head, and dragged myself forward of the van feet first. Jackie saw my face restyling efforts and decided to ring for her dad to take me up to the Minor Injuries department at the Hospital. I sat down in the kitchen and waited.

The next thing I knew I was waking up on the floor. My first thought as I came round was "what a funny place to sleep, I must have been absolutely ragged last night". I honestly thought it was morning and I had no recollection of thumping my head with a spanner until several minutes later. The mind really can play some odd tricks sometimes.

Being owners of a vehicle with a large carrying capacity meant that we got involved in ferrying various groups around. David, our son, was involved in the local under twelve's football team and also ran for the local athletics team. Jackie was the local Brown Owl, and our girls all went through Brownies.

Being involved in ferrying young footballers around led to assisting with the training. Some things the lads were good at, but football was not one of them. Some things I was not good at, I kept finding out to my cost. For example, one of the exercises to improve agility was to run forward until a designated line marking was crossed, then turn and run backwards, all done as quickly as possible. The trainers were expected to take part of course, to show how it should be done. I gave them a head start and ran for the line like an Olympic sprinter. By the time I hit the line, they were all turned around and running backwards, I was determined to beat them to the edge of the pitch.

Now logic says, you cannot run anywhere near as fast backwards as you can going forwards and I was about to prove the point in style. As I turned, inertia took over, my backside went down and my legs came over my head, not once but twice. But I was not the only one who didn't make it to the far end of the pitch. Now freshly and thoroughly coated in mud, I looked up from my worms eye vantage point, all I could see were creased up miniature footballers, none of them had made it to the far line, but theirs was not an inertia problem, more a problem of uncontrollable hysteria.

In one particularly bad home match, our lads were losing 0 – 14 and one of the other trainers, who will have to remain anonymous, decided to allow the subs on without taking any players off, now this was done quietly and one at a time. It did make more of a match of it for a short while. But it was obvious that there were too many players on our side of the pitch when the teams reassembled after goal number 15 was scored. The air was blue, the opposing team captain completely lost it (can't say I blame him) and was threatening all types of sanctions from the league and a few from God! However a warning from the ref about bad behaviour on the sidelines saved the day, the 'spares' were withdrawn and the result stood. We lost 0 – 17. I did think that we should have put all our spare men in goal.

On one occasion, we were returning from a match in the van, celebrating a draw against one of the other struggling teams, when there was even more noise and hilarity than usual from the back of the van, we had just passed a crowd of girls at a bus stop and I assumed that it was something to do with that. *It was*. Three of the lads had perched themselves on the back seat, dropped their pants, and were mooning at the assembled crowd of young ladies.

I uttered a few words beginning with 'b' and they clearly understood how I felt about them blocking the view in my mirror.

The van got used for other outings besides Holidays and transporting sporting groups about. David had wanted to go to a basketball match and take a few friends for a birthday treat, and we obliged. We took nine friends, all boys, and with David and myself there were eleven. The van was still comfortable but was almost at capacity. The England versus Denmark match was excellent, and as a final treat we stopped on the way home at Brian's Fish and Chip shop in Headingley. We all bowled out of the van into the chip shop, and each and everyone of the lads got mushy peas and chips in a tray. As I was paying for the food the till operator called me over for some quiet advice, "I should wind a couple of windows down if I were you", he whispered thoughtfully.

We made good use of the van, and went on many excellent holidays, but sadly it met its demise while we were travelling across North Wales. We were on our way to Abersoch for a holiday at the time, and we were brought home by a rescue truck. We bundled what we could in the Astra Estate and set off again! What a squeeze!

The van engine refused to budge, It was a complete seizure. I think I stripped the engine down out of curiosity, because by now the van was very weary and not really worth saving. Bizarrely, there was a pound coin embedded into the top of one of the pistons! There are some things that really cannot be explained!

9
Magnets and Clusters

I am a Design Engineer by trade, and of course this means that have spent the majority of my working life in an office. All types of offices, from great big open plan affairs to tiny little back rooms. There are always characters in any office, some of them full of their own importance, some funny and some irritating. You can always see little political victories, and disasters. There have been times in my office life where I have opened my mouth and put my foot in it.

We used to have a drawing office manager, Roger Priest. Roger was a small chap, very old school, very smartly dressed, always well spoken, never raised his voice in an open office, but was quite willing to give you a severe ticking off behind closed doors. Roger's shoes had steel tips on the toe and heel, I suspect, not because he was mean, but more likely because they were very expensive.

Roger would emerge from his small office at the end of the drawing office and do one circuit past everyone's desk before returning to his paperwork. He had a particular way of walking, very slow and deliberate and always absolutely the same speed. Even with the large drawing boards we had in those days you could tell when he was approaching by the slow clip, clip, clip of his shoes. Colin, one of the other draftsmen, had found that he could imitate the walk, which he often did on a Saturday morning in preference to doing any work.

One particular Saturday morning, I was in thinking mode.

OK then, I confess, I had my feet up on the tray under the drawing board and I was leaning back in my chair, staring at the ceiling in an absent minded sort of a way not doing anything, when I heard Colin doing his finest impression. "Shit", I started loudly ,"Roger's here, I suppose I had better do some bloody work."

The footsteps stopped. You could have heard a pin drop. I looked across the office to see Colin hard at work at his drawing board, looking at me open mouthed, with terror on his face. A head peered around the drawing board. "Yes" Roger said, "I suppose you better bloody had!" It was the only time I heard Roger swear and the only Saturday morning he ever worked!

How on earth I got promoted to be in the design team after that I don't know, but I was, and I finished up in a much smaller office at the end of the drawing office. The only problem was that the clock was now on the opposite side of the wall, and I had no idea of the time, but I found timekeeping was easy because when it was lunchtime or home time, the lads in drawing office would all make a move together to get their coats on. Someone must have worked out how I was doing my timekeeping, because one day, as the drawing office moved in unison to put their coats on, I went for mine from the cloakroom at the back, put it on and stepped out into the Drawing office to find that they were all sat back down working. I still had over an hour to work!

As a design engineer, I was under the expert eyes of Robin Banks. Robin always expected you to give a precise reply if he asked you a question, and if he felt your reply to anything was less than utterly complete, he would ask something like, "when you say the unit is large, what *exactly* do you mean?"

We had had a couple of large magnets stuck to a cabinet in the design office for months, and I had taken these around to Robin's office for strength trials, and now I was returning them to the design department. As I walked through Drawing Office, I was pushing the two units together with like poles at the same end, like a silent accordion. I have no idea why I decided to turn one round, but before I had completed the turn, the magnets took over, and clamped a substantial piece of my hand between the faces. There was a fair bit of power there, and as I tried to pull my hand out from between, the magnets got closer together. The closer they got, the stronger their grip. I finished up running the last bit through the drawing office, and grabbing a screwdriver from my drawer, which by now was an essential tool in the quest to extricate my hand. I finished up with a huge blood blister. I stuck the magnets back on the filing cabinet, and there they stayed.

On the top of the filing cabinet was a box of cereal, a sort of clusters thing. This had been sent by an American customer who was after a machine. It turned out that these were delicious to eat straight out of the box, and I have to confess, I had a couple, as did everyone who worked in the design department. The box stood there for weeks before Robin rang up from his office, and asked me to come round to his office and bring the box of cereal, as we needed to discuss the job.

As I picked up the box I had a sinking feeling. Some kind person had left just one of these clusters in the bottom of the box. I stuck my head around Robin's office door and said, "I think you might be a little disappointed".

"What *exactly* do you mean when you say disappointed?" came the reply. I mustered up courage to shake the box, but not to enter the office. "bring it in" said Robin with a hrrmph! We held the meeting about this multi- million pound project with a single cluster on the desk in front of us. I am sure he knew that the box had been raided before I got called over, Robin was a shrewd cookie. I am also sure that I was getting the blame for scoffing the lot, and the solitary cluster on the desk was Robin's way of making a point.

Robin's boss was Angus Hall. Angus was a Scot, and I think Robin resented the fact that the board had seen fit to bring in Angus above him, but Angus had been put in charge of Electrical as well as Mechanical design. Robin had never been able to see eye to eye with Dick Taytor who ran Electrical and Angus's job was, I think, amongst other things to get the two departments working together.

As often happens when you are designing bespoke machinery, we had had a job which had gone wrong, and there was to be a crisis meeting about how the situation could be rescued, and as usual we had to wait until all the main players were in the office together.

Angus saw me in the corridor, discussing the job with a couple of the draftsmen and asked why I was not in the crisis meeting. I replied, "Because the crisis meeting is this time *tomorrow*." There was no apology. He frowned before turning away and walking towards his office.

"You want to get your f**king act together" he said as he marched off briskly, clearly in a bad mood.

"Bugger off Angus", I said under my breath, once he was safely out of sight.

Unfortunately Angus had excellent hearing, from somewhere the distance he shouted, "Did you say something?" Suddenly there was a scampering of feet and I was on my own in the corridor.

"I said, I wondered if you were feeling a bit off Angus" I replied. I kept my job.

10
France

I have to admit, we like France, or at least the bits we have seen so far, and I don't care what anyone says, there are a great number of very nice French people, who are willing to help out when you are struggling with the language or any of the strange customs, like shutting the shops for two hours on a lunch time. Unfortunately this still leaves over forty million of our Gallic Chums who are surly Brit-haters. Oops – I must apologise for that straight away, some of them are willing to struggle to understand the thickest Glaswegian accent just to prove that it is the English they despise, not the British.

In 2003 we decided to travel down to the Dordogne in search of warmer climes. We (the holiday four) had booked a caravan and the plan was to drive down and back in nice easy stages, taking a day in Paris on the way down. We duly arrived at Portsmouth and had waited in line until the Customs men were ready to check us all through. They were pulling cars to one side at random and parking them at one side of the main stream of cars for assorted random checks. We got pulled over.

The customs officer asked me to get out of the car and follow him with my passport. I was instructed to open the boot. The trusty old Astra was on its knees with the stuff we had packed and the customs man could clearly see that if he chose something from too low down in the pile, the boat would have to be delayed. He chose a harmless looking backpack from the top of the heap, and asked me to follow him with it. From somewhere behind me I heard Jackie's voice say "Where are they going with the picnic bag?" The hair on the back of my neck suddenly stood on end. The picnic bag. He could have picked any of dozens of bags, but he had to choose the picnic bag!

I placed the bag on the conveyor, and it set off in the direction of the x-ray machine along with a couple of other bags from other unfortunates who had been chosen. When it got to our bag the conveyor stopped, there was a huddle around the screen. The officer who had chosen the bag spoke. "Bloody hell, there's a bloody *arsenal* in here!".

Someone came across and took my passport and disappeared into a small office. I was called around to the screen. There were corkscrews, knives, can openers, steak knives, all in full view. "It's me picnic bag" I whimpered.

Visions of being hauled off for a strip search quickly flashed though my mind, along with spending the first night of our holiday in jail on the wrong side of the channel. The conveyor started and when the bag emerged I was asked to open it. By now there was no one around apart from me and half a dozen customs men. Someone came out of an office carrying my passport, smiling. Discussions around the cutlery came to a conclusion.

"Don't take it out of the car on the boat, sir, and have a good holiday".

Visions of Police cells melted away. Outside all the other cars had gone. The bag was buried in the boot under several others. "I thought you had been arrested, what happened?" Jackie started.

"They saw what was in the bag and gave me the full treatment." I replied

"What? You mean…?" questioned Dawn

"Yep" I replied, "Latex gloves, the lot! Now let's get on this bloody boat before it leaves us behind"

The following day found us in Paris and we did a real whistle stop tour of the city. We found a parking place underground near the Arc De Triomphe, and after a quick look around, caught the Metro to the Eiffel Tower. Another brief look around, (we chose not to join the long queues to go aloft), then it was across the road to get on a boat upstream to Notre Dame.

After Notre Dame we set off in the direction of the Louvre, but there was a strike, so we headed for the Montmartre instead. Having looked around the artists markets, and the Basilica, We headed off down the hill, stopping for a beer, and eventually for a wee in an electronic street loo. There must have been a fault on the electronics on the one I tried as the doors opened and closed about four times behind me, as I stood there relieving myself, to the amusement of Jackie, Tim and Dawn and the local population.

By now things were getting busy for the afternoon rush hour and on the Metro on the way back to the Arc de Triomphe we were packed like sardines. A smartly dressed gent squeezed in to the doorway, he had his expensive looking jacket over his shoulders, but did not have his arms in the sleeves. I was soon to find out the reason.

The train sped up and then began to slow as we approached the next station. In the crush I could feel the movement of a hand down around my trouser region. I immediately thought "Oh my God ! I'm being touched up by a pervert." *[personal reminder – must go and seek psychiatric help when I have time.]* I moved my hand down with the intention of crushing the offending hand, expecting it to be attached to a particularly limp wrist, only to find that there were fingers tightly clasped around the top of my wallet, tugging. The hand rapidly disappeared, as did the gent, because he had timed his move to perfection. The doors opened and without a sideways glance, he stepped out backwards on to the platform empty handed.

I made a grab for the corner of his jacket, with the idea that I might stop him or at least deprive him of his jacket. I missed by a mile. I smiled at the thought that my fat arse had prevented the thief from removing my wallet undetected, and then at the thought that, If he had been successful the wallet would have been removed from his grasp at high speed as the train set off, still attached by the chain to my belt. Jackie asked what I was smiling at, and I explained the guy in the jacket had just tried to steal my wallet. She gave me a puzzled look. "I thought he was touching me up" She gave me a really puzzled look. I smiled again at the thought of what might have been if I had managed to grab and keep hold the jacket.

Once back at the car, we were on our way, I had looked at a map of Paris and worked out that we needed to go south to find the A10 so that we could head for Orleans and that, mistakenly as it turns out, there was a ring road, other than the new Motorway Periphique which would do the trick.

Oh dear!

The old 'Route Periphique' is an instrument of torture, not a ring road. If you can manage to stay on it and not be accidentally diverted off down a side street, there are dozens of roundabouts. Huge, wide, busy roundabouts with no road markings. The typical Parisian driver has a special technique to deal with these roundabouts based, I think, on the fact that once on the roundabout, the average speed of a vehicle is nil. The technique consists of hurtling at the roundabout at high speed and jamming the brakes on once you have found a gap. The gap does not need to be the length of a car. The width will do, leaving your car at right angles to the intended travel of everyone else. With the first part of your plan in place, sit with your hand on the horn until the cars in front move far enough for you to do the necessary to get your vehicle pointing in the correct direction. Ah! Such technique! No wonder the cars of these French commuters look like they have been rescued just in time from the crusher.

We stayed over in Orleans, and we really pushed the boat out and stopped in a Formula one Hotel. For those of you who are unfamiliar with the genre, it's a Hotel for us poor folks, seriously cheap, you won't be interested.

When we finally arrived at our destination we went to the reception armed with our paperwork. The nice lady behind the counter explained that we must see the man called Shim, and showed us on a map of the site where we would find him. Shim was outside his tent, milling around, he was a short wiry little man, and had obviously spent a lot of time in the sun. He wore a green vest and huge Khaki shorts with turn-ups that looked as though they had had far too much starch. His skinny brown hairy legs, on the ends of which were a pair of huge dusty boots, hung down from the corners of the leg holes of his shorts and only just reached the ground. He approached the car as we got close. He had an enthusiastic, bouncy, gym teacher sort of a walk.

"Are you Shim?" I asked "Nay lad, I'm Jim, and whereabouts in Yorkshire are yer from?" Jim replied, having immediately recognised the accent through my deliberate, slow English. Jim explained he was from Garforth and would be here if we needed anything. I am sure that he would have been. Jim showed us to our caravan which had everything we needed including our own bit of grass and a barbeque.

The evening was warm and we decided we would sizzle a bit of meat on the barbie and have some salad with it. I was sitting there in the warm evening sun, with a glass of Stella feeling thoroughly at peace with the world, well almost at peace, I had gas. Now, an open camp site is not the sort of place where you want to hear an Englishman farting loudly. In any case, being English means that, unlike other Europeans who are allowed to ignore the fact that they have farted, to let rip is either a cause for utter shame, or hysterical laughter, depending on the mood of the company around you, oh, and of course whether you follow through or not. I chose to dispose of the offending methane having first hidden myself away in the caravan loo.

Dawn was in the kitchen, washing the salad and caravan walls are very thin. I figured that if I rested one buttock on the toilet seat I could allow things to pass silently. No. There was no rasp, no trumpet blast, but instead of silence there was spectacularly loud hissing noise rivalling anything that a steam engine could produce.

A voice came from the kitchen addressed at Jackie and Tim "This is going to be bad. he's using the spray before he starts"

2003 was the year that there was a heat wave in France, and I consider that we were fortunate to be there just at the beginning, and not in the worst of it. However, it did get to the stage where Tim tried Dawn's bra on his head as a sun hat, and I have to say, it was a perfect fit, but somehow Dawn felt that this was not an appropriate thing to be wearing no matter what the weather, I suspect it could have been the fact that the unused cup did look a little foolish hanging down Tim's back.

The week was a scorcher and there are dozens of things to do in the Dordogne and some surprising things to learn about the way we lived in the past. I thoroughly recommend Roc St Christophe, the chateaux at Beynac and Castelnaud and the walled hilltop town of Domme. There is a wonderful forgotten village just west of Sarlat, but it's name escapes me!

11
Summat else

Yorkshire folk are proud of their native 'tongue'. Lets face it there are still places in Yorkshire where the accent is so thick that it is somewhere between dialect and a Yorkshire language. We [the holiday four] have on occasions used this fact to no avail whatsoever, but had great fun laiking about with it.

We had planned a trip to Brittany, and as usual we drove, got the ferry and then took a steady run down through France. I had found us farmhouse lodgings from the internet, near a place called Dol De Bretagne. We had called in at Mont St Michel and so arrived at the farmhouse quite late. As we pulled up we saw the daughter of the farmer, who was about twenty sitting on the doorstep, smoking. At the side of her was a bucket containing every cigarette butt that she had discarded since she was twelve. She did not speak English, nor did her parents. We were shown our rooms.

A deeply domed, small round brass light switch illuminated a forty watt bulb, which hung in a heavy beige lampshade with brown tassels. The room was very darkly decorated, with bare floorboards stained in a dark oak colour. An ancient bed, about three feet tall with huge dark oak ends, stood in the middle of the room, adorned with sheets and dark brown hairy looking blankets, and covered with a brown candlewick bedspread. The wallpaper, which was changing colour with extreme age, was a rather fetching green and beige pattern of vertical stripes about two inches wide. Huge dark oak wardrobes stood at either side of the bed, and under the shuttered window was a dressing table with a bowl and a huge ornate water jug. I wondered for a second if there would be an ancient chamber pot under the bed, to make the room qualify for en suite, but there was a door off to the left which led into a Victorian bathroom, with a very old but at least a proper sit down lavatory. The flush was facilitated via a battered lead pipe feeding down from a wooden box. Dawn and Tim's room was similar in décor and had a door on the right leading into an identical bathroom to ours. So identical that the battered lead pipe had identical dints in it. Clearly there would have to be a system of knocks to gain entry for late night pees.

We did not hang about, we did what we needed to do and headed off to Dol to find a pub.

In Stewarts Bar we ordered drinks and were quickly joined by a local called Jan Konit. Jan was a character, a Breton, he insisted in speaking English to us as he "Didn't like the bloody French" and anyway he had "Learnt our bloody language very bloody well" and he was "going to make sure he damned well bloody used it" Bizarrely, Jan produced a battered photograph from his pocket of the Queen presenting him with some sort of medal. He was obviously very proud of his encounter with "your bloody Queen" but he would not explain and we did not push it. I did wonder however if he had had a conversation with her.

It was the feast of St Michael and locals were going around the bars with food and distributing it to everyone. We had a wonderful evening.

Waking the following morning we opened the shutters and found we were looking out on to a cornfield that stretched for miles. You could visualise tin-hatted Tommy's coming out of the corn, and I wondered if the room had been redecorated since those days. I concluded that perhaps it hadn't.

A hearty breakfast of home made jam and home made bread later we were on our way, heading for Pont Aven. Once we were booked in and installed in our caravan we went down into Pont Aven village for a Crepe. I saw something on the menu that I had never had before and so I ordered it. I did think it was a little strange when the waitress asked me if I knew what andouiette was, to which I replied that I thought it was some sort of sausage.

The crepe arrived, covered in pigs intestines. *Note to self*- throw away that handy little French English Pocket Dictionary.

The evening found us in the bar at the camp site we looked at was on offer, and then had a discussion about what to get, and then about how to order it. I went to the bar and in my awful French ordered three beers and a cider and then something in my head clicked and I said to the barman "Tha mun avail thissen o summat anorl"

"Na then" ,came the reply "yer English is ok, yer French is crap., and I'll 'av a Stella ta" I never used the French again at this bar as it was staffed entirely by Brits, all of whom could speak French (although some better than others). We nicknamed the barman who served us 'Morley' because that is where he was from. The fact that not a single one of the bar-staff was French was much to the disgust of the French customers, who *really* took exception to it. Marvellous! I did order the odd drink in broad Yorkshire just for the hell of it.

12
Unruly Clothing

I have never been the worlds tidiest dresser, this is not to say that I am a slob. If I do make an error in selecting my attire, I am deeply embarrassed and self conscious about it. The fact is that my brain cannot function early morning to the point where I can organise a suitable set of clothing for the day's tasks. Little surprise then to find that as I was going along the Fruit and vegetable aisle in a busy Asda store one morning, a sock began to appear from the bottom of my trouser leg.

I was immediately in a quandary, do I make it look as if I am selecting something from the bottom shelf and secretly pick the sock up? If I do, and this move is caught on CCTV, would they think that I was stealing something as I sneakily pocketed the offending item of minging footware? I would then be dragged off into an office somewhere and forced to empty my pockets when, horror of horrors, yesterdays sock would make it's re-appearance again on the managers desk.

I considered the alternatives, I could, for example, stand on the thing and drag it out from the trouser leg without bending down, and then kick it under the shelf, where it could lay undiscovered until the hygiene team were called to deal with the putrefying lump under the shelf. No one would be any the wiser as to its origins, thinking it to be rotting vegetable matter or similar.

I looked down at the sock. It's position on the wrong side of my shoe would mean that I would have to do a manoeuvre resembling an Irish Jig in order to extract it by standing on it. I didn't want to appear drunk and anyway, it was a good one, no holes, no thin bits. I plumped for the option of pulling the sock out and pocketing it. I did the rest of my shopping thinking that at any moment I would be approached by a security guard and hauled into the office.

My mental bleariness on a morning has resulted in a few faux pas when it comes to clothing. One in particular will haunt me forever.

I was at one time blessed with the task of reporting the progress of Research and Development work to the board of the company I worked for. The same meeting would consider new ideas and proposals for inclusion in the program, as well as my plans as to how accepted proposals could be handled through the company. This task meant that I would be spending the whole day in a meeting surrounded by suited up gents. This did make me try somewhat harder on meeting days, and with my chief organiser's (Jackie's) help, I would in general fare quite well. Unfortunately this takes a little longer than crawling out of bed into the first item of clothing, therefore things tend to get rushed towards the point of having to leave. This particular morning Jackie reminded me that I would require a clean handkerchief (there is nothing worse than pulling a crusty rag out of your pocket to blow your nose on – is there?)

I rushed upstairs and pocketed one quickly from the drawer. It didn't matter that it didn't feel particularly well ironed as long as it was nice and clean. The meeting was in full flood and mid morning found me wanting the handkerchief. As I got the thing to my face I realised something was wrong. Under my nose was a pair of my four year old daughters pants. My immediate reaction to this bizarre discovery was to sniff the nose drool back in instead of blowing my nose on the pants. I then screwed the pants up in my hand and re-installed them quietly in my pocket. I looked around at the assembled gentry. The bored expressions of a few minutes previously were still fixed on most of the faces, but there were now a few raised eyebrows and a wry smile.

Surely if they saw what happened they would realise that this was an error of judgement in selecting the correct drawer in the dressing table.

Surely they realised that if was in the habit of sniffing ladies undergarments, that I would not have chosen this particular forum to give a demonstration of the methods involved. My voice faltered slightly as I continued.

No one has *ever* mentioned the incident, I have therefore consoled myself with the thought that none of them could have seen it.

I think.

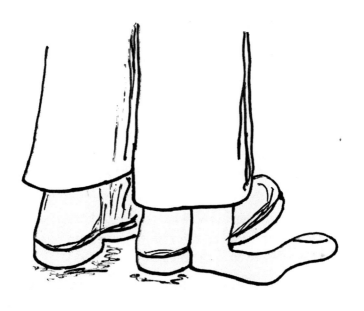

13
Little Red

We had always fancied a little sports car, and had dreamed of maybe getting a Morgan one day, but some things are always beyond your grasp, in particular when you have been busy bringing up a houseful of children, each with their own interests and requirements. The kids had always come first and although we never managed to scrape together much in the way of pocket money, they never went short. We had put our sporty aspirations to one side while they were growing up, but one day found ourselves, as many parents do, home alone.

Jackie had been fingering through the local paper when a picture caught her eye. There was the car of our dreams, a bright red, old fashioned sports car, looking for all the world like a Morgan, what is more, at a price that we could just about afford. It did sound far too good to be true, but we rang the number anyway and arranged to go and look at it on the following evening.

The car belonged to a gent called Mick Itteka living somewhere in Cleckhudmondfax, [for those who have never been, this is an area south of Leeds and Bradford where all the towns run into one another] and we were given a long set of instructions on how to get to the house, which we followed carefully and only got lost a couple of times. When we finally arrived, typical Yorkshire February weather had set in big style. Little Red was duly uncovered and stood there with the light of a dozen reflected street lamps glistening in the rain off the highly polished red paintwork. "Wow!" I thought, and I turned to look at Jackie, who had clearly fallen in love with the glistening beast in front of us, my brain continued silently, "it looks like I am parting with some brass, 'cos there is no way I am going to get out of this one – not even if it runs like a dog"

Once we had given Little Red the best look over we could using torches an avoiding kneeling in half an inch of slush, we went for the obligatory test run. I scrambled into the back, Jackie sat in the front and the gent drove. Little Red behaved itself. I started to clutch at straws in order to save a few bob. "Gearbox is a bit noisy" I said.

"Yes", the gent said, "and there is no synchromesh on first gear which takes a bit of getting used to, but you have to expect this, it is the genuine original 1964 gearbox and engine after all, but it **has** been fully reconditioned."

"Bugger", I thought , "He's proud of his noisy gearbox! He's even made it sound like a selling point!" I looked around desperately for a leak in the soft top – nothing! I gave up trying to win points.

So there we were ten minutes later, proud owners of a traditional British sports car – a Moss Malvern.

[?] We were soon on our way. My first problem was that even with the seat fully forward, I was having to control the pedals with my tiptoes, this hadn't been a problem for the previous owner as he was about six feet three. His problem was more one of getting access to the drivers seat, he appeared to have to dislocate his neck to get it in under the soft top, and he did admit that having owned the car for three years, he had just mastered the art of getting in and out. My current problem was partially solved by placing a huge block of wood under the back of the drivers seat in order to tip it forward. - Please don't ask why I keep a huge block of wood in the Astra, I don't think I actually know.

There are large swathes of this area of Yorkshire that appear to be devoid of any form of direction signs, it could be that none of the roads actually go anywhere, or that no one ever expects anyone who is not a local to venture in. The upshot was that we got thoroughly lost, and the first time we, that is me in the Moss and Jackie in the Astra, picked up a road sign we were several miles in the wrong direction, the right road, but the wrong direction. A swift U turn sorted the problem out. We were soon on our way, but what happened next was unexpected.

The road from Cleckheckertyhudhousefax to Leeds passes through several valleys, and on the first uphill from one of these, Little Red spluttered to a halt. We hadn't even got back to where we had started from! Jackie duly pulled up behind in the Astra, and got out to enquire about the problem. Little Red immediately started again and we were soon on our way.

The same happened on the next hill, and the next and the problem seemed to be getting worse. We tried spraying the entire engine compartment with damp start, to no avail. Every time we stopped, the engine would restart, and we were soon on our way again. I began to suspect that there was no air getting in to the petrol tank, but releasing the cap didn't produce any rushing air noises, and in any case, it was definitely getting worse. It was now very late, very wet and a sort of a cold dampness that only occurs on winter evenings north of Chesterfield was starting to lower our spirits. Euphoria to despair in an hour, it is amazing how quickly things can go downhill. The next hillside and the next investigation with a torch revealed an in line fuel filter, hidden down the back of the engine. In desperation I decided it had to go. I had a short piece of nylon tube in the Astra [don't ask] which was duly fitted instead of the filter. We were soon on our way. I was filled with dread as we approached the next uphill section.

There was no splutter, no coughing, Little Red shot up the hill, Jackie flashed the lights of the Astra in celebration, and we continued back home without stopping, save for the odd red light here and there.

Once things had settled down and we had got used to the fact that we were now the proud owners of a little red sports car, we had to take stock of what we had bought. Nothing on Little Red is as it seems, it is a real sheep in wolf's clothing. Basically the engine and chassis are a 1964 Triumph Herald 1200. The rest is a mixture of Ford parts and other spurious bits. This means that to get any spares is a bit of a lottery, and it is useful to know someone who can identify stuff. We had to do two immediate modifications before we could make use of the Moss. One was a heater, off a Seat something or other in the scrapyard, the other was somewhat cruder and quite essential, three inch block extensions to the pedals so that someone of a normal stature had a chance of bringing the vehicle to a halt.

Winter faded away into spring and we were eager to go out with the hood down. The spare wheel on a Moss is centrally mounted on the outside of the car at the rear, and two of the press studs that hold the soft top in place had been cleverly positioned behind the spare wheel, meaning to put the top down involved loosening the spare on its mounting. This done, the hood was neatly rolled up around the folding frame and we set off - alfresco. We were a mile down the road when Jackie thought she had heard a bump. "I'm sure something fell off then" she said.

"Bloody hell, don't look now," I replied, "we're being followed!" There, about ten yards behind us and travelling at the same speed as we were, was our spare wheel. It didn't take long to realise that we couldn't stop and grab the thing before it did any damage. In fact we couldn't stop or slow down at all! Our fate was entirely in the hands of our spare wheel and the laws of gyroscopic science. Luckily after what seemed an age [and before the STOP sign at the end of the road], friction and gravity took over and the wheel did a pirouette in the road behind us. Seconds later a car pulled up behind us, the driver got out and presented us with the large aluminium retaining knob from the centre of the spare wheel. "I saw this drop off and I stopped to pick it up, but when the wheel followed it, I thought that I had better give you plenty of room."

"When the wheel followed *us* I thought that *it* needed plenty of room!" I replied, "thanks for that, sorry to be a trouble"

"Oh, no trouble" he said, "It was fun to watch"

I bit my lip. Jackie kicked my ankle. "You never tightened that up after you did the hood" she snarled

"I think I may have been a little unsure about how tight it should have been, I didn't want to damage the tyre" Jackie kicked my ankle. "Ok, ok, I forgot to tighten the bugger up" I confessed.

We were soon on our way.

14
Dunni's Café

When we were teenagers we were Mods, well sort of Mods. We ran about on scooters, wore parkas and hung around at Dunni's caff. Dunni's is a wonderful place, a haven for two wheeled vehicles of all persuasions. We used to spend quite a lot of our evenings there in the late sixties, playing pinball and drinking disgusting coffee. Occasionally we would discuss going out for a run and then set off at a moments notice up the dales or to one of the seaside places within easy reach. Being centrally placed between the two coasts, we would count Blackpool, Morecambe, Bridlington, Filey or Scarborough as such places. We were a little ambitious on occasions, especially during times of the year when the weather was less than reliable.

One evening we had one of these discussions, and decided that it would be a laugh to go to Morecambe, as there were lights on at that time of the year. There was a park called Happy Mount Park at the north end of the town where they had light shows that rivalled Blackpool. Clearly we had not thought this through in its entirety. It was at least half past eight when we decided to set off, and in those days the A65 up through Skipton was far slower than it is now.

We arrived as Happy Mount Park allowed the last visitors out through it's gates and locked up, so we decided to have a walk through the illuminations along the seafront. It was not very long before the streets were deserted and we set off back towards the scooters. We laughed about Morecambe being a 'dead hole' and 'having to stand their dead in the bus shelters to make it look busier'. But we couldn't help thinking how strange it was that we were the *only* people about. Spooky stories were banded about, and very soon we had worked ourselves up into a sort of apprehensive mood.

Then we found out why the place was deserted. Every single light went off bang on midnight. Such a sudden change in the amount of light leaves you with 'feel' as your only way of finding your way about. It seemed to take an age to find our scooters, we were grateful for the odd insomniac's window throwing a bit of light so we could see the path. We couldn't wait to get out of the place before whatever 'night creatures' the locals were afraid of got us.

As we set off 'Pop' Hanson said that we would need to look for somewhere to get some petrol on the way home. This did seem to be another bit of bad planning, as the nearest all night petrol station was probably sixty miles away in Leeds. Sure enough, he spluttered to a halt near Gargrave. To make matters worse it was starting to snow. Wet horrible stuff. We pondered on how to get petrol from one tank to another, and decided that the hose from Pop's air filter to his carburettor would make a suitable container, and if it got ruined then it was his hard look for getting us all frozen stupid. We disconnected it and used it to transfer a small amount of fuel at a time into Pop's tank until he had enough fuel to get home. It is amazing how cold your hands get messing about with petrol on a windswept, sleety Yorkshire hillside at 2am.

Blackpool was our favourite destination, though and we spent days there or camped overnight. One Easter we decided to do just that, and a group of about six of us set off with about as much camping gear as we could carry considering the fact that we were on two wheels. Which is not much!

Pretty quickly things started to go wrong. We had Just got through Skipton when my engine started making a loud clicking noise. I found out later that this noise was my piston rings disappearing through my exhaust port in tiny pieces. (If you are technically minded – yes they can – on an old fashioned two stroke) This resulted in a loss of power and an inability to run at low revs, but a short stop and a restart in the car park of The Coronation, a roadside refreshment spot, convinced me to continue to Blackpool instead of doing the sensible thing and returning home.

We installed ourselves in a camp site just outside Blackpool. Two of us were sharing a tiny pup tent. Four lads next to us had managed to bring a much larger tent, how I will never know.

We spent the afternoon wandering around the Pleasure Beach and going on the occasional ride. I went on the Wild Mouse for the one and only time in my life, and convinced myself that I was going to die. I managed to hold on to my lunch until I got off the ride and then decorated the pavement with it.

The evening finished off with a hour or so in Diamond Lil's Saloon with light hearted banter across the room between ourselves and the Bradford Scooter Club. When we emerged from the bar, I tried to kick the Lambretta into life and failed. I finished up running with it and then dropping the clutch, after what seemed like a hundred yards, the scooter fired up and we made our way back to the camp site.

The night was cold and so were we and the last thing we needed was one of the lads from the tent next door testing how waterproof our tent was by relieving himself all over it. It wasn't. A fine mist sprayed through on to us and the air, as well as being damp and smelly soon became very blue.

Breakfast was strange. We had managed to pack cereal, milk and spoons but no bowls. Somehow eating handfuls of cornflakes and then swigging milk just did not appeal in the same way as sitting in the doorway of the tent with a bowl of cereal would have done, and anyway the box was soggy and I was unsure about the origins of the soggyness. The four lads in the tent next to us had decided to head for a café for breakfast. We swigged the milk off then opted to join them.

The scooter resisted all attempts to start. Using the method from the previous night, I pushed it up and down the camp site to no avail until I threw up. Diced carrots and milk! (There is always diced carrot).

We had to wait until the other lads got back from breakfast, and by that time the tent was packed away along with everything else. We kindly donated our urine soaked box of cornflakes to the four lads in their absence and we hoped that they would enjoy them. On their return, one of the lads offered to tie a rope between his scooter and mine with the idea of towing until mine started up. We failed. After dragging the scooter round the site several times it was obvious that it was never going to splutter into life. Someone told us that you could transport a scooter on a train and we decided that this was how we were going to have to get home.

We were faced with the problem of getting my stricken scooter approximately five miles to the station, much of it through the streets of Blackpool. Again a tow was offered and gratefully accepted. Now, I am sure that this must be illegal, and if it is and you are a policeman, then I have made this bit up. If it isn't illegal, then it is something that in any case, speaking from personal experience, should **never ever** be attempted. Apart from the fact that being towed caused extreme stability problems, I was being towed through the busy streets of Blackpool by a lunatic whose only concern was to drop us off as quickly as possible and get on with his holiday. The tow job made the Wild Mouse look tame. I was so relieved at the end of the journey that if I had had anything left to throw up I would have made it a hat trick of pavement pizzas. We rang up my dad and arranged to be picked up from Bradford Interchange and then wheeled the scooter full length of the train to the 'Guards Van' where there was a ramp to aid us across the gap.

A short journey to Bradford saw us on another platform, doing the same in reverse. We were quickly loaded into my dad's Austin A40 Countryman. Top bloke my dad.

Now the technique I was using to try and start the Lambretta was not quite 'bouncing' the bike off, this technique involves running with the bike, in gear, but with the clutch held in, then leaping on at the same time dropping the clutch and letting inertia take over. The engine will then turn and hopefully start. Easy eh? If you get it slightly wrong the results can be disastrous.

At one time Jackie and I both worked in Guiseley, and I finished work 15 minutes before Jackie, so I would ride to Jackie's work, we would meet up and ride our scooters home together. On one of these occasions Jackie's scooter would not start and I offered to bounce it off but Jackie is very independent and wanted to start the scooter herself, she had done it before and knew exactly what to do, but as she went to leap on, she stumbled. With the clutch now released the engine fired up, Jackie was dragged down the road. To stop yourself bashing your face on the ground in this situation, you have to hold on, and the thing you are holding on to is the throttle, plus there is no time to think. In Jackie's case she was dragged about the length of a cricket pitch at an impressively horrific speed before the scooter hit a lamppost and stopped abruptly. Jackie kept going and went from being dragged along the floor to being airborne. She landed unceremoniously several yards in front of the lamppost. The horror unfolded in front of dozens of work colleagues, and myself, and Jackie was quickly surrounded. I think Jackie's pride was hurt more than anything else, it certainly didn't dampen her enthusiasm for scooters, she rode mine home! Jackie's was a write off, thank goodness it was the scooter that hit the lamppost!

Jackie and I had a habit of stopping to help scooter lads in obvious need, I think it made us feel good that we could usually sort problems out for people. This was principally because we had had all the problems ourselves and we made damn sure that we had tools and other essential bits with us when we went anywhere.

On one occasion we pulled over to help a scooter lad having obvious trouble changing a wheel. I had a modified socket which was much better than the pathetic pressed steel effort that came in the Lambretta toolkit whose only purpose seemed to be to create a nice rounded edge on the corners of any wheel nut it was used on. The socket did the trick, but as we were changing the wheel a group of about forty motorbikes came by, blowing horns and laughing at the misfortune of a scooter having to have it's wheel changed.

Our new friend took exception to the jeering and made a huge 'v' sign at the group. Suddenly he didn't feel like a friend anymore as the bikes all turned round and quickly surrounded us. I started to think about which side we should be on, when the leader of the bikers pulled up close by us, and lifted his visor. It was Alan Drover. Both Alan and his dad worked with me, and Alan's girlfriend was Jackie's best friend. Without a word he signalled for the baying mob to leave us. Thank goodness for friends, even if they were Rockers.

The atmosphere was a bit cooler now, I think the

guy realised that he may have been a little hasty with his hand signal. We finished changing the wheel and the lad thanked us. We wondered what for, helping out with the wheel change, or saving him from a kicking!

Certain evenings of the week you would find us at the Motown club, a local youth club. The club had a certain amount of street cred, partly because of the fact that there were several of us with scooters and we would all be there at the same time. The club was held in an old school building, which had a stone playground wall all the way round. On dry evenings we would sit on top of the wall facing the main road and talk, or just watch the world go by. In those days I was a bit more athletic than now, and I fancied myself as a bit of a jumper. Teenage lads are show offs sometimes and I thought that I would be able to run, and jump and turn at the same time and, without putting my hands down, land with my backside on the wall. This would show all the other wimps, whose method was to face away from the wall and do a sort of reverse push up until they were installed at the top of the wall.

It didn't show the other wimps up. I certainly got enough height to get on to the wall but unfortunately I was travelling at quite a speed. The wall stopped the progress of my legs, but allowed the top half of my body to continue. This put me in a rearward spin and I finished up face down in the playground wondering if I had just survived an earthquake. I think that my little manoeuvre had an impression on the wall sitters. Most of them laughed until they cried. And I had to suffer the indignity of people (particularly girls!) remembering the incident and bursting forth with laughter every time they saw me for weeks.

15
DIY Disaster Area

I have to admit, I am not the best at DIY. I somehow lack a bit of finesse. This is not to say that I cannot put up a shelf, or assemble a set of drawers. But somehow things go wrong from time to time, and I finish up bruised or covered in something.

When we first got married we moved into a Victorian back to back house on Ilkley Road in Otley. Most of the house was decorated in woodchip and painted white, but the hallway, which was very small, had a sort of leather effect embossed wallpaper on the bottom half, and many dozens of layers of paper on the top half. We chose to redecorate this tiny corner of our newly acquired abode. We had bought just enough paper to do the job of course, Jackie was doing the pasting and I was doing the measuring, cutting and hanging. Jackie brought me the first piece of beautifully prepared, pasted length of wallpaper, neatly folded concertina style. As I stepped on to the ladder the bottom end of it unfolded and I put my foot through it. We had a choice. The paper was very cheap because we bought the last two rolls, so we could either hang the damaged paper or abandon the project until we got some more paper. We chose to hang it. So there it was, our first attempt at hanging wallpaper, with a foot sized semi circular rip facing us every time we came in through the front door.

It is unusual for the wallpaper, or the tiles, or the floor covering to come off worst out of my many battles in the DIY arena. It is usually me that suffers some damage or other. One time we had decided to remove an old stone shelf from an old pantry, This thing was built into the wall on three sides and was constructed in reinforced concrete, and there wasn't room to swing the hammer properly. Several blows into the removal job with the lump hammer and I caught the knuckles of my right hand on the edge of the stone shelf as I brought the hammer down, not once but twice. The first time I did this it really hurt, the second time it *really really* hurt. The air was thick with words that begin with 'F' and 'B'. I did a little war dance around the kitchen and decided to go back into battle with the shelf. Not wanting to chance the same thing happening a third time, I swapped hands.

The angle I had to stand at to do this was really awkward and I had to place my right hand on the shelf to steady myself, and with my weight steadied thus, I could take a big hefty swing with the lump hammer. This I did but as I brought the hammer down I caught my left elbow on the door frame, and the hammer came down square on the already throbbing, skinned knuckles of my right hand. This time I danced around for a bit longer. In fact it was a couple of weeks before I put my head inside the cupboard again. I came to the conclusion that I should put my right hand inside a safety boot before I took one more swing.

I am really not built for confined spaces, and I think that in any case they conspire against me. We had a slight leak in one of the valleys in our roof, and I decided that this could easily be cured from inside the house using expanding foam. Access into this area is a bit limited but I jammed myself into the corner and aimed the nozzle between the felt and the tiles and gave it a good hearty press. It wasn't long before I realised the error of my ways. With the canister now put down, for the next five minutes or so, foam oozed from every gap and hole in the felt, and formed stalactites, which then became too large and heavy to support their own weight, these then fell on to the semi captive me below forming stalagmites all over my prostrate body. By the time I had managed to extricate myself from my loft prison, the stalagmites had turned into large flat, very, very permanent foam pancakes.

Not that my disastrous exploits are confined to enclosed spaces I can quite as easily come adrift out in the open air. On one occasion I was up a ladder, one of those three section aluminium ones, painting the fascia under the gutter. A nice blue colour, naturally I was being very careful, not leaning out from the ladder, which meant that I was up and down the ladder with the pot of paint, you would think that after about twenty times of doing this, I would have got the idea. Nope. Descending with the pot of paint in my left hand, I missed the rung below the joint in the ladder and slid the rest of the way down, with my stomach bouncing against every rung, and clinging on to a pot of blue paint as if it could arrest my descent. When my feet hit the floor, the paint decided that it had been in the pot for long enough and I was coated from shoulder to knuckle. Nice blue colour though. Long lasting formulation too!

16

Belgium

We don't, of course, always go to France if we go abroad although, if we use the ferry it almost always means that we land in France and travel onwards, and whilst we think that there is something special and unique about the towns of Ghent and Bruges we wanted to go further afield and we plumped for the Belgian Ardennes, calling in at the French border town of Valenciennes on the way for an overnight stop and Ghent on the way back to the ferry.

We travelled from Dover to Dunkirk and then drove up the coast road, not the motorway as we had plenty of time to look around, until we hit Belgium. We hit Belgium ok but the road disappeared after about a hundred yards. Without any warning sign in sight, other than a barrier across the road, the whole road surface had been removed to a depth of about four inches, presumably to make the section cobbled. During our stay in Belgium we were to discover that this was typical of the Belgian attitude to road works.

We followed the border in a sort of general south easterly direction and eventually crossed back into

France near Valenciennes. In the evening we walked into the town centre for a meal, the first place we stopped at we were ignored by a surly French waiter so we moved on and had a wonderful meal just a few doors down. We were entertained by a group of musicians (never in a million years) whose playing was so truly awful that people gave them money to clear off. One of the group had a trombone and despite his best efforts with the slide, the note that came out of the end of the instrument was always the same pitch. He did try to make an effort with the length of the notes and on a couple of occasions you could just about make out what tune the sound he was making was supposed to be. The drummer had no idea that the thing he was bashing was supposed to beat some sort of time to go with the music. He must have thought as long as he made a random noise with it then this was ok. ---- It wasn't.

As we walked back towards the hotel we saw the musicians (never in a million years) being angrily ushered away from a pub doorway. We were not surprised, but we were amused.

The following day we circled Valenciennes in the car looking for Belgium, which considering that Valenciennes is about four miles from the border, is a masterpiece of the French sign-makers art. In typical French style, almost anything that is over the border is relegated to 'Autres Directions'. One exception to this strict rule is Brussels, so this is what we followed in the certain belief that once we were over the border into Belgium we would pick up the signs and then be able to head in the right direction.

We arrived at La Roche early in the afternoon, a pleasant riverside place in a deep narrow valley, with the ruin of a Medieval castle sitting over the town. The weather was warm and did some exploring then had chips. We got some supplies from the local Spar supermarket, including a bag of Barbeque coal before heading to the site.

Late afternoon we were at the campsite and we checked in, we were shown our caravan. Caravans are not known for having large toilets but this was the tiniest room I have ever seen. So small in fact that you had to reverse in if you wanted to do a sitting down job. This removed the loo roll from its hanger, so we positioned it on the cistern. Problem with this was that when you were sat on the loo you couldn't turn to get the toilet paper off the top of the cistern. I joked in the bar later that I had needed to fish behind me for the toilet roll by reaching over my head holding the loo brush handle, jamming the brush into the hole in the centre of the roll, and that to open the door all you needed to do was break wind!

The following day we tried to get a barbeque from the camp office, but these had all been put away as this was now the end of the school holidays and high season had finished. While we were out we purchased a disposable barbeque from the Spar shop, and when we got back we lit up, but before we threw the sausages at it, we decided to top it up with some of the barbeque coal we had purchased earlier. Removing the mesh grill proved to be a bit on the tricky side to say the least, quite possibly the fact that we had already lit the barbeque wasn't too helpful. I did think that it seemed a bit of a heavy bag for its size, and the reason became clear. We had bought coal, ordinary fireplace - in – the – house type coal.

We spent the week exploring the area and even went into Luxembourg to the Chateau at Vitrac. One of the high spots of the week was the Grottes de Han, for about ten pounds each we were taken on a train ride around the back of a mountain and up a valley, where the train stopped by the entrance to a cave. We walked for about two kilometres through the cave, stopping part way in a giant chamber where there was a light show with music and eventually getting to an underground river where we got into boats and floated the rest of the way to the exit, close to where we caught the train. This is well worth a visit.

At the end of the week we had a visit from the spoon Gestapo, who counted all the cutlery and checked that you hadn't left a turd in the bed before giving you the deposit of 150 euros back.

On the way back to the ferry we stopped at Ghent, this is a wonderful old low countries town, full of canals, old traditional buildings and drinking and eating places [just our sort of place actually]. We went out in the evening to the old part of town and had an excellent meal before retracing our steps alongside one of the canals to the hotel.

The following morning we felt as if we already knew our way around and we did a bit more exploring. There was a square near the church that had street entertainment going on and we stayed and watched for a while. I spotted an interesting building down one of the side streets and we wandered down to look at it. I managed to get us thoroughly lost by walking the wrong way up one of the streets on the way back to the Hotel, so lost in fact that we had started to panic about getting to the ferry in time. We solved the problem by catching a tram which took us back to somewhere we recognised. Back at the Hotel we didn't waste any time getting our stuff together and going! In the end we made good time and even had time to stop at the border tobacconists shop, purely for our own use of course.

On the boat back from Dunkirk, we found a nice table in the bar and relaxed, an old couple sat at the table behind us. He settled down to read the paper. **_Out loud!_** And every single story he read started with the words "It says here……..". We got the impression that this was the first paper in English he had seen for months. After story number fifty I was about to get up and strangle him, but after his little introduction to his next little gem of enlightenment: "It says here….." ,his wife who was clearly as fed up of this as we were said loudly "Oh **_do_** shut up, Edgar you old fool!" The rest of the crossing was peaceful!

17
Chocolate and Chips

A company that I worked for at one time in my career made mechanical handling machinery for the food industry, I used to get to follow the whole thing right through from concept to installation and commissioning, so I got to see plenty of interesting useful ideas, as well as other peoples utter disasters. You should know that large scale production is generally automated these days despite the rural, stone-baked imitation world that we see in TV advertising, and that a good many ovens have a wide metal (or even stone) conveyor running through them, and can be hundreds of feet long.

We had a contract to replace a disaster installed by another automation company at a 'famous cake company' in Corby, but the programme to complete the installation would mean that we had to work long hours to avoid disturbing production schedules. The mechanical part of the installation was quickly finished during the first day. We had had to work until ten pm but we were feeling very confident about finalising everything on time. We called in at the chip shop on the way back to the hotel. I have to say they looked particularly nice with crispy knobbly batter and nice yellow crisped up chips. I didn't fancy the idea of walking through reception at the Hotel with my wrapped up cod and chips, so I hid them in my briefcase. On the way up to the room we had a quick get together in the corridor about the following days work.

I got into the room and started a bath running, I was aching all over and I figured a nice hot bath would sort out my aching bones. It was wonderful settling down into the bath after the gruelling and very long day we had had, but as I lay there relaxing I caught the hint of a familiar smell. Fish and chips! How did I manage to forget! The hunger came over me suddenly and I had no choice but to get out of the bath and get them.

I unpacked the wonderful smelling concoction from my briefcase and started to unwrap them as I made my way back to the bath. With one chip already in my mouth I entered the bathroom thinking what luxury, fish and chips in a hot bath. I hadn't reckoned on just how slippery the bathroom floor was, my feet went forward and my wet backside slapped down on the bathroom floor, I recovered from suddenly being overcome by gravity and weighed up the situation, there were chips to my right and chips to my left, but not many, I had managed to cling on to the vast majority. The fish was nowhere to be seen. I raised my stinging red backside from the lino and sat forward to peer over the edge of the bath. There it was! The flipping thing had made a last bid for freedom and was slowly rotating around in the bathwater.

By now, not only was I psyched up about the forthcoming luxury, but my posterior had just had a serious slapping, so I was not about to let either the fish or the bathwater go to waste. I extracted the fish and several dozen of the crispy bits that were floating around, and resumed my bath. I have to say the batter was not quite as crispy as I had imagined it would be.

The following day we were all togged up and back into it, white coats all round and paper hats, and me with a snood on my beard. Putting together the electrics took longer than we thought, we had done no preparation work and we finished up working until the early hours to get the job done. Andy, the electrician we had taken with us was bending a piece of stainless steel tubing and managed to knock the lid on a huge vat of chocolate, which had been sitting there right next to where we were working, stirring away all weekend. The stirrer on the vat immediately stopped and, try as we might, we couldn't get it started again. We decided to wait until Steve, the bakery engineer, came around. Two hours or so later and the electrics were finished and tested. Steve came by to see how work was progressing, and we confessed about the chocolate vat. He soon got the thing started, but a skin about two inches thick had formed on the top of the chocolate. The motor turned and there was a huge quacking noise as the newly formed skin parted company from the chocolate beneath. The newly formed giant circular chocolate bar lifted the lid as it gyrated and stopped the machine. Chocolate flowed down the outside of the vat and formed a layer in Andy's toolbox, where it immediately set on everything it touched. We were in hysterics at the sight of chocolate pliers, spanners and screwdrivers exactly like the ones you can get in a traditional sweet shop, but with slightly harder centres.

With all the motors tested, all that was left to do was to load a program into the machine's computer and things would be ready to run. I offered to stay behind and finish off while the other lads went to grab a couple of hours sleep. It was now early Monday morning and the place was starting to come to life. I had my head inside the control panel when the leads of my voltmeter disappeared like scampering mice from under my nose. I looked around to see my toolbox, laptop and the voltmeter with wire dangling, trundling down the bakery on the conveyor which had up to now been a handy workbench!

With the new oven un-loader up and running, production was starting, unbaked cakes were being loaded in at one end of the conveyor through the oven, the other lads were back from the hotel having had about three hours sleep. I stayed just long enough to see the first products out of the oven and then set off to the hotel to get my head down, leaving everyone else on standby for the day. I was desperately low on fuel, so I called in at the garage on the way, I thought that I was getting some strange looks when I went in to pay. As I climbed in to the drivers seat I caught sight of myself in the rear view mirror wearing a rather fetching, brown hairnet style snood on my chin.

18
Fuel

People tend to do unusual things when they have had a couple of drinks. Some get involved in fights, some fall asleep and some just simply turn out to have a very silly side. I tend to do one or other of the last two and in this respect my son in law, Mick, Tim and I have a lot in common.

We had decided to celebrate the forthcoming marriage of Becky (my youngest daughter) and Mick in traditional style and go down into town and get bladdered. Otley is still an excellent place to do this despite the demise of many local pubs in recent years. The problem was that at about ten o'clock, Mick (who still appeared stone cold sober to the rest of us) went to the loo in the Ring of Bells pub and never came back.

We searched the immediate area of the pub, there were alleyways where he might have gone to sleep, walls he might have climbed over to bed down. Bit by bit we went further afield, it was cold and it was raining. About 1 am we set off back up home, about one and a half miles. Where the road gave a choice of two routes we split up. The river was a roaring torrent, and all sorts of things started to go through my mind. Was he in there somewhere, floating seaward? Or had the little bugger had a change of mind at the last minute about marrying Becky? Was he laid out somewhere in a drunken stupor, getting himself a serious dose of hypothermia?

Home got closer. Becky's car was outside and I started to wonder what I was about to tell her. Whatever it was she would almost certainly be distraught. I peered through the windows of the car in the faint hope that Mick might have got in and fallen asleep. Not a sign, if only we knew where he was.

Becky was asleep but Jackie was still up, I explained the situation. We decided that it was worth having another look around. Another walk into town, Another long scour around, and a walk back by Green Lane all proved futile. I was wet, cold and thoroughly depressed. It was almost breakfast time when I gave up, went home and sat down with a cup of tea, some bloody good night out that was. Becky came down as I poured out my cornflakes, I asked if she wanted something, thinking I would get her comfortable before giving her the bad news.

"Morning Pops, morning Bex!" announced Mick as he came in through the back door "Flamin' cold out there! What's for breakfast?"

"Where the bloody hell have you been?" I shouted.

"Don't shout at Mick!" Becky interjected.

"Slept in the car"

"No you bloody well didn't, I looked" I replied

"Don't swear at Mick!" Becky interjected.

"In the boot, it was open"

"You are f**king well kidding me aren't you."

"Stop swearing" Becky interjected.

The anger began to subside, not only would Mick have known where we keep the spare back door key, but it wasn't locked in any case! He did look somewhat dishevelled and cold, serves him right. I went to bed eight or so hours late, happy that he wasn't floating out to sea.

We often go down into town on an evening to sample life and the local beers, these days we have got a bit lazy and more often than not if we have missed the last bus up home we ring for a Taxi, but there was a time when we would walk home after an evening session whatever the weather was throwing at us. One stormy evening we had just passed the end of Green Lane when we saw a large branch blown down in the road. We have an open fire at home and this looked like a superb find. "Can't let this fuel go to waste Tim" I said. "I think you are absolutely right" replied the equally as daft Tim.

We dragged the branch along Weston Lane, it was a considerable weight. The odd car went past. Some blew their horns at us and we waved. We passed the O'Deigh's house and dragged the branch around the corner to our house. Luckily the car was not in the drive and it had been parked so that we could manoeuvre the branch around and drag it into the drive. We were exhausted, but we felt as if we had achieved something.

The following morning in the cold light of day, I could see the enormity of what we had done. Our drive is long enough for two or maybe three cars at a pinch, but not quite long enough for the huge lump of tree that was sitting there for all to see. I wondered if we had broken any law by collecting it. We certainly must have broken a few road traffic laws dragging it home.

New Years Eve must be top of the list when it comes to drunken exploits, simply because there are more drunken idiots about. We used to spend New Year at home when the kids were small simply because of the difficulties of getting a baby sitter, and we would see the new year in with Jackie's Mum and Dad and then bid them farewell at the gate in the early hours. On one such an occasion we were saying goodbye as our neighbours, Jimmy and his Dad were arriving home. Jimmy is disabled as a result of a bad accident at work and walks (unsteadily) with a stick. He was having to support his Dad who had obviously had a few too many. The seemed to be getting on alright until the old man tripped over the kerb and fell full length, spark out. Before we could offer any help Jimmy had gone over to the window to arouse the attention of his Mum. Unfortunately he used the stick to knock on the window with a little too much enthusiasm, and the entire pane was soon on the living room floor. Jimmy's mum was a large Irish woman who didn't pull her punches when she was riled, and boy, was she ever riled! With the longest and loudest string of expletives I have ever heard, she manhandled the two inebriates into the house, each held tightly by the scruff of the neck. I think the old man didn't even wake up for this indignity, or perhaps he thought it best to appear not to.

These days we tend to spend New Years Eve at the Social Club around the corner. Sometimes Jackie's brother Stan and his wife Carol join us along with a whole host of friends, and they will walk to Jackie's Mum's house, about a mile away, at the end of the evening. One year we had just arrived home ourselves, the time was about 2am, when the phone rang. Stan was on the line. "Ah! Glad you're still up, can I call in and get a key for Mum's house? I've lost mine"

"I'll come and meet you part way so that Carol doesn't get frozen waiting for you" I replied. I set off with the key in hand and got to the football pitch at the bottom of the street. Stan came marching around the corner and as he went past my hand holding the key out to him he wished me "Happy New Year!". I thought that it would be interesting to see how far he got before he realised that he had just walked past me. At about twenty yards I realised that he wasn't going to be turning round. I shouted and he stopped. As I ran up to him almost in total surprise he said "Oh, Hi! I'm just going up to your house for a key for Mum's"

I stood there and frowned at him. He frowned back, but I could see the thought process taking place albeit very, very slowly. "Ah!" he said "that's Mum's key isn't it? Thanks….. Dohhhh"

"Dohhhh!" I thought as he turned and went.

19
Courses and Exhibition(ism)s

I have been fortunate enough to have been given the chance to go on an assortment of training courses, and to visit exhibitions, which can also be very educational. On the odd occasion, I have helped to man the stand at an exhibition. This is far from being educational, It can be one of the most boring jobs ever invented, and despite the tedium you have to be enthusiastic if there is ever anyone on the stand who hasn't come just for a freebie pen or peanuts. To make matters worse, all the time you are trying to get people interested in your products, they have already had a quick look and learned all that they wanted to in the first three seconds, and the last thing they want is to be pestered by every idiot potential salesman who thinks that he has managed to land a new client.

We were sharing a stand with a Dutch company at a four day exhibition. I had been there to help set the stand up and then travelled back home. The first couple of days had apparently been dire, with hardly anyone attending and even fewer showing interest. The boss had decided that he had had enough standing around and I was appointed to take his place in the sure and certain belief that since there was no interest whatsoever, there was nothing for a rough arsed Yorkshireman to foul up. I did my best to drag people on to the stand but the words apathy and futility kept coming to mind.

So there I was at the end of the exhibition, a quick dash round in the last five minutes meant that I had enough ball point pens to last the next three years, and then the big strip down began. Alan turned up with the van and we soon had everything packed up apart from the fixtures and fittings, which included a little office/kitchen. I said goodbye to the remaining Dutch guy, Karel [nothing to do with superman] who had a plane to catch, and then made my way back to the remains of the stand to get my coat from our little office. When I got back there was no sign of the coat, it wasn't a particularly special coat but it did have my car keys and wallet in it.

Straight away I reported the loss to security, no one had handed anything in. Walkie talkies crackled everywhere and tannoy messages rang out around the hall. Nothing had been found. I resigned myself to the fact that I had been robbed. I rang the bank to report my cards missing. Then I rang the AA to help me sort my car out. A very nice man came and it took him two minutes to get into the car which was quickly put on to a trailer ready for the journey home.

A couple of days later, back at work I had a phone call from Holland. "Hello, we have something of yours here" Said the well spoken Dutch lady.

"Oh, what's that?" I said.

"Erm, your coat" came the slightly nervous reply.

"You are kidding" I said,

"Erm, no, one of our guys picked up your coat thinking that the other one had left it behind"

"Well, I do feel like an international jet-setter" I said.

"Why is that?" came the reply.

"Lunch in Birmingham, Dinner in Otley, Luggage in Amsterdam" I said.

"Sorry" she replied.

Most of the courses I have been on have been more enjoyable and interesting than the dire exhibition, with the possible exception of an all day talk I attended on 'Strict Liability and the Law'. I think the mistake was that a hearty lunch was provided, and afterwards we had another long session. In the middle of the afternoon, one of the assembled throng was clearly struggling, and started to snore, very gently at first, but eventually so loud that the poor guy giving the lecture had to stop and ask someone the wake the sleeping gent up. I was glad that he went first, not me.

Of the courses I have attended one of the more interesting was one run by the Smallpeice Foundation, this taught us how to do lateral thinking and how to apply it. There were team workshops and interesting lectures, with application techniques, plenty to keep us occupied.

After the day's work, I wandered back to a nice little Bed and Breakfast a mile or so up the road, and went to my room for a shower, before going out for a bite to eat. The bedroom had a sliding door into the bathroom, which had an electric shower unit mounted on the wall to the right, by the door. A bath with a bracket above it on which the shower head was mounted was in front of me. To the left against the wall under a half frosted window was a washbasin, all fairly standard stuff.

I didn't bother closing the door in to the bedroom as I stripped off to get into the shower. (This might have been a bit of a mistake.) There was only me to embarrass. I threw my clothes on to the top of the bed through the open door and got into the shower. I lathered up my hair, but as I did I caught the shower head and the water stopped coming, With my eyes now full of suds I did my best to quickly wipe the soap away to investigate what had caused the sudden interruption of my ablutions, to find that the shower head was no longer attached to the bracket, and was now swinging back and forth like a pendulum, attached to the electric shower unit by it's flexible hose, soaking first the bathroom floor, and then my bed with my recently abandoned clothes in a heap on top and then back again.

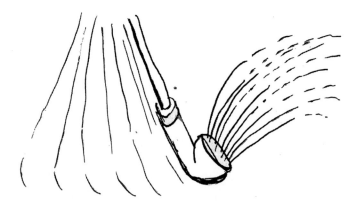

I jumped out of the shower to rescue the situation, still covered in soap suds, grabbed the shower head and pointed it at the gap in the shower curtain to prevent any more damage being done. Whilst all this chaos was happening, a double decker bus pulled up at the traffic lights outside. Over the top of the frosted section of glass, and only about fifteen feet from where I stood, a woman was peering over the top of a pair of reading glasses, grinning at the antics of this soapy lunatic. (*If this was you and you are reading this, Hello there!- Erm – what you observed was probably as a result of my room being too cold!*)

20
Pies

One of our sister companies used to make machines for producing apple pies, and we made ovens and coolers which allowed these pies to be made in vast quantities, fifteen lines, side by side, and a row every couple of seconds. When you see these lines running, you have to wonder to yourself how could they possibly all get eaten.

As usual with these things, not everything had gone to plan, and the oven had been taken up to temperature but the packaging machinery was still not in place. We had a team on site and wanted to prove our end of things, so we persuaded the bakery to make up sufficient quantities of pastry and sweet mincemeat to allow us to do a meaningful test. We had a bit of experience in making this type of pie and made a good stab at what the oven settings should be.

Soon there were about forty rows of pies heading down the oven conveyor, as they came out of the other end, baked to perfection and smelling wonderful, everyone started to think of food. It was getting towards 1.30 and the bakery canteen was about to close. Suddenly I was on my own. The pies entered the chiller and then trundled onwards. After the chiller was a long cooling conveyor and then .....nothing. All six hundred pies were heading like lemmings to the end of a conveyor where they would fall on the floor in a great sticky heap.

There were some cardboard boxes at the side of the conveyor and I grabbed one and started to fill it. Just as things were starting to look futile, a couple of operatives off the next line turned up and started to help. Soon all the pies were safely installed in cardboard boxes, not the six packs that they are normally sold in, but a couple of hundred to a box. I thanked my temporary helpers and left the boxes by the end of the cooling conveyor.

We worked late into the evening to get everything completed, but eventually we got to the point where nothing else could be done, I went to see the bakery engineer to tell him we had finished. I told him that there were a couple of boxes of pies by the end of the cooling conveyor.

"Take them" he said quickly. ***Result!*** Two of us were travelling home in the same car and we split the loot. The freezer was full and I ate mince pies until I was thoroughly sick of the sight of them. I have still never figured out whether the engineer thought I meant a couple of six packs.

A few days later we got the call that the packing line was ready and we made our way back to the bakery to help get things into production. With the bakery manager in attendance, a short run of forty rows was planned. As they came off the pie machine and headed towards the oven, he flicked the switch on the sugar dusting machine and turned it off. "Not wasting sugar on a test run, they are only going to the pig farm" he said.

He was there at the oven mouth as the pies came out, the few minor adjustments we made after the last run meant that these were perfect. "Right", he said, "get them in boxes, we will send them out to the markets as seconds"

There is nothing like money, I thought, for making you change your mind about something.

Quickly we were into production runs and the sugar sprinkler was turned on, but standing at the end of the chiller, I noticed that every couple of dozen rows, there were pies missing from one edge of the conveyor. I went to the gap between the oven and chiller and there was a continuous stream of pies, so they were obviously finding their way off the side of the conveyor inside the chiller. I peered down the tunnel expecting to see the effect of too much air flow, after a few seconds, a pair of hands grabbed two pies. There was someone inside the machine, squatting at the side of the conveyor, helping themselves. Exceedingly nice pies though!

21
Livestock and Pyrotechnics

I have never been a great lover of animals, I am including *some* pets as well as farm animals in this. For a number of years the nearest I got to farm animals was when fireworks were on sale and we used to blow up cow clap with bangers. The sloppier the better, don't try this at home of course and you need to keep well back, It does take a bit of explaining if you are too close when the firework goes off.

When I was an apprentice I had a close encounter with warm cow clap and I cannot recommend it. I used to travel to work on my scooter ,down a country lane which has a couple of dairy farms on the way, one of the farms is on a bend, and if you get there at the wrong time, the cattle have resurfaced the road with the brown sloppy stuff. I got there at the wrong time one morning and there was a fresh coating. Of course I was travelling too fast to get a grip on the glistening slop and I finished up on my back and absolutely covered. Undaunted I re-mounted and continued on to work. When I took my helmet off my hair followed it upwards, like brown fingers from the back of my head.

The back of the helmet had a generous coating inside and out, and the smell was rank. I was sent home on full pay for a bath.

For a while I worked for a company whose offices and workshop were on a farm. Phil Barrows, the farmer who runs this small affair, keeps chickens and unusual breeds of sheep and pigs, which he breeds as well as selling the produce such as organic eggs and meat. One year the old sow had given birth to about eight piglets. We had brought some of the grandchildren to see these when they were tiny and in the pig shed, but now they were in an enclosure in the middle of the field by our office window with a little corrugated iron hut in the centre. At least that is where they should have been, but Phil's battery had gone flat on his electric fence and this allowed mum to make an escape bid, along with eight little offspring that still followed her everywhere. Phil and a couple of assistants struggled for about an hour, dragging, pushing, shouting, even trying to use a door to steer the sow in the right direction. But she was large and strong and had other ideas. Nothing would persuade her to go back into her little pen. Having watched the drama for a considerable amount of time, I came up with a bit of a plan. I went down into the canteen and opened a pack of smoky bacon crisps.

I went up to the sow and fed her a crisp. She followed me towards the enclosure. The piglets followed their mum in a long straggly line behind yours truly. I dropped a crisp, and then another and when I was in the enclosure I emptied the entire bag. I was the sow's best friend ever. Phil was dead chuffed as well. Neither of them seemed to mind the fact that the crisps were smoky bacon flavour. I hope it didn't invalidate anything about organic produce.

Some encounters with animals come as a surprise rather than by plan, our youngest daughter, Becky had been lucky enough to be involved in making a short film which was shown at the South Bank, and we went down to see the screening and the presentation of an award by Keith Chegwin. I chose to park the car near Primrose Hill, and we walked to Camden Town, where we caught the tube. The screening went down well and there was more applause for the film made by our little group than any other. It does give you a buzz. After the ceremonies had finished we retraced our steps and stopped at a Macdonald's in Camden to celebrate.

I volunteered to walk to where the car was parked and come and pick everyone up, so I cut directly across the park at Primrose Hill. On my way across I became aware of a dog in the distance, three or four hundred yards away, a large, nasty looking thing, probably a Rottweiler. The beast was running as fast as it could towards me. I was determined not to be phased by this, and continued to walk as if nothing was happening. When it got to a few yards away I was convinced that I was about to be mauled. It continued on its path and so did I, until it ran into my legs and I spun in the air. The dog continued in a straight line. I picked myself up and looked around to see if anyone had seen my downfall. They had. A posh female voice from the distance shouted "sorry!", I waved in silence, utilising less than a full complement of fingers before dusting myself off and continuing on my way, aware that the dog was now on the opposite side of me to its owner.

I presume it had had it's fun as it didn't make a second attempt on my dignity.

Another encounter we had with livestock of a different kind came in the days before we had opened the fireplace out. We had noticed a smell in the front room and presumed that milk had been spilt into the carpet and no one had confessed. We desperately needed to clear the air and to this end we used shake and vac, and then carpet shampoo, but the stink was still there.

There were a couple of large flies buzzing around, but when I opened the window they made a bid for freedom and I thought nothing of it. It did seem, over the next day or two that every time we went into the living room there were another couple of these very large flies to deal with. We searched and could not find the source, and things were gradually getting worse. Then came the solution we were looking for. A fly crawled out of the vent at the top of the gas fire. Within minutes the fire was disconnected and pulled away from the chimney. Now there were hundred of huge flies around the room. A dead magpie lay on its back in the fireplace, the feathers on its stomach were gently undulating up and down under the pressure of hundreds of maggots, and the smell was appalling.

I quickly went to the shed and got a seaside bucket and spade to deal with the bird before it walked again. I gave it a thoughtful and considerate burial, it was rapidly disposed of in the bin! Since then we have made sure that if this happens again, the bird will become fuel rather than maggot food, as we now have an open fire.

Now the open fire is not entirely without problems. We tend to burn wood if we can in preference to coal, and you cannot always guarantee the dryness of the logs. This led me to try to rekindle the fire one day using barbeque lighting fluid. *[Do not try this!]* After squirting an inordinate amount of the stuff on to the pathetic embers, all I had managed to do was create a large amount of light grey smoke, until it lit. The flammable smoke ignited all at once with a pink flash and a resounding boom. The fire was lit but the hearth was now full of soot. I was on my back, devoid of eyebrows, on the living room carpet. Outside it was snowing inordinate quantities of black soot. I chose not to enlighten any of the neighbours as to what had caused the layer of black dots on everyone's cars and washing. I guess it cleaned the chimney though.

I suppose the most idiotic thing I ever did involving fire was to burn my mothers washing line. This was a plastic coated line with a metal wire rope core. I cannot remember what caused me to light it, but the result was a spectacular light and sound display. The line burned for a few seconds and then a burning drip formed, which made a roaring noise as it headed for the ground. It took a good half hour to burn from end to end and it was a wonderful display to watch. As the last drip hit the ground I started to wonder how I was going to get out of this one. Instead of a washing line was a soot blackened wire. Despite racking my brain I failed to come up with an excuse, not that *any* excuse would have got me out of the mire, and I got a clip around the ear, grounded for a week and made to pay for the new line out of my pocket money. That was about as bad as it ever got at our house!

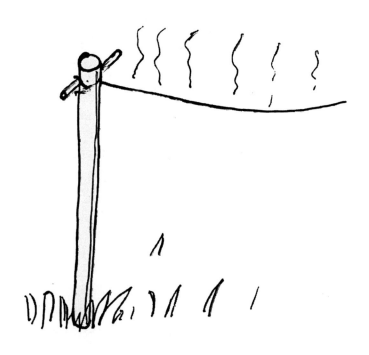

22
More about Chips

Sometimes when you are commissioning bakery equipment, there are things which happen that you could never have envisaged in a hundred years, and there are others which should be so obvious that you wonder if you or those around you would easily pass an 'A' level in gormlessness.

We were testing a newly manufactured box stacking machine for a company that made microwaveable chips, and in order to test the thing, some of the guarding was left off, and only skilled and sensible engineers, who understood the ins and outs of the machine were allowed near it for safety reasons of course. I knew the machine better than anyone, because I came up with the concept and design, so why I did what I did will remain a mystery to me forever. We had a problem that every so often the machine would stop for no apparent reason. I suspected that there was a problem with the photocell detecting that the boxes were actually in to the machine, so I reached in through the inlet mouth and deliberately put my finger in front of the detector.

How dumb can you get! The machine detected my

finger and immediately indexed what it thought was a box sideways off the conveyor, it wasn't a box of course it was my hand, luckily still attached to my arm, but now well and truly stuck in the machine. I looked around at my co workers and there was terror on their faces. The pusher, which was now well and truly bent, was clamping my hand down into what used to be a 5mm gap. I shouted for someone to get a screwdriver to ease the pusher up so that I could get the remains my hand out, which they did with little delay thank goodness. My only injury was a deep groove across the back of my hand, the skin was not broken but it was obvious that a second index of the pusher would have removed all the skin from my wrist to my fingertips. There was no blood, just a bruise. I have to say that this is without a doubt the stupidest thing I have ever done, and the closest I have ever come to losing a body part. I still cringe when I think about it. It did teach me to treat machinery with respect.

After the job had been up and running for a few weeks, I had a phone call from the engineer. The machine would apparently run for twenty minutes or so without a hitch and then stop for no apparent reason two or three times before the problem cleared and then it would be ok again. The operators had discovered that if you pushed the boxes back down along the conveyor, the machine would start up automatically, and were therefore doing this several times an hour to keep the line running. I was run off my feet with other work and I ignored the first call to go to site completely. When the second call came through, a few days later, I had to think fast. I told the engineer that I had been studying the program for the last couple of days and thought that I had found the problem. He insisted that I come over to sort the program modifications that afternoon. I gathered up my equipment and set off to Scarborough. As I drove I pondered over what the problem might be, it could only be that the photocell on the inlet conveyor was struggling to see some of the boxes. The boxes had a lot of black on them, and the photocells struggle with black, as I had already found out in the hand trapping exercise. But why this had not occurred before, while we were commissioning the line I could not figure.

By the time I got to the factory, I had everything worked out in my mind to change the software to solve the problem, it was a sort of a software bodge, and it literally it took seconds to reprogram, but it worked instantly. We watched the machine together for a while and then the engineer went away with the plan of coming back later for a report on any problems. The machine ran faultlessly. On his return he enquired if there had been any problems. I replied that everything was still going ok.

"Wonderful, absolutely wonderful, great!" he said . I was dead chuffed that my efforts were appreciated, "You **Bastard** why didn't you do that days ago" he continued. It was the shortest moment of glory ever.

While watching I had noticed that every twenty minutes or so, but at random, a few boxes would come along the conveyor the other way around, and these were the ones which my software bodge was having to deal with, when they got to the photocell a black part of the box lined up with the beam. I followed the conveyor to a point where there were weighing scales and a desk with forms full of figures. An operative turned up and removed three boxes from the line, weighed them, inspected the chips, and put them back on the line. He was not particular about which way round they were. "*You* bastard" I thought, and then collected my gear and set off for home.

I once had to visit a chip factory in the north of the Netherlands, about four km north of a little place called Roodeschool, if you have an old map you will find that there is nothing but North sea four km north of Roodeschool. The journey there was notable for a couple of reasons. On the day we were to set off I had worked the morning, because we were flying to Schipol (Amsterdam) airport on the evening flight. I had my lunch and then walked into town in my lunch break and was on my way back to the factory when I heard the receptionist on the tannoy calling my name and asking me to contact switchboard urgently. This I did. The girl on the switchboard told me that the evening flight was cancelled, and that we had to make our way up to the airport straight away as the afternoon flight was at 2.30pm. Considering that it was now 1pm, and it would take us half an hour to get to the airport and the check in time was 1.30, this was quite a tight schedule!

I rang Jackie to get her to pack my bag, which we picked up on the way to the airport. Amazingly we made it to the check in desk in time, but we were about to be disappointed. The check in clerk told us that there had been some technical problems and the estimated time for the afternoon flight was now 4.30pm. We were offered a free meal on KLM airlines which we accepted.

4.30 came and went. We went to the desk to be informed that they were still having problems and there would be no afternoon flight. We were offered a free meal on KLM airlines which we accepted. Angus Hall had earlier been concerned that because we were booked on the evening flight, we might be late into Amsterdam and had arranged with the hotel to make dinner reservations. 6.30 came and went, we declined the free meal offered, and at 7.30 we boarded the plane, surprisingly only one hour late.

The KLM flight came with all the trimmings, there were drinks on offer and food, which we pushed around with our plastic forks. We duly landed and got into our hire car for the journey up to the northern tip of Holland. When we arrived at the hotel we were presented with plates with the largest steaks you have ever seen, smothered in pepper sauce, I forced most of it down!

A road ran north from Roodeschool across the barren plain of a new polder. The grass was sparse but there were a few sheep dotted here and there. We came to a 'T' junction and turned right towards the chip factory. At lunch time we went to Otto's café. This was a Portakabin at the other end of this desolate road. There was not one other building in the area. Otto was a large rotund man with a grubby blue and white pinafore stretched over his ample belly. He sold egg and chips, sausage and chips and pie and chips and the place was a goldmine. Perhaps this was due to the fact that Otto had a captive clientele. When we asked Otto what there was to do on an evening, he waved a huge grubby finger in the direction of the sheep, I think he meant it.

The low countries have chip factories from end to end. At the very opposite end to Roodeschool, on the French border with Belgium I had an experience I will never forget. We had developed a freezer that could be run continuously, when I say a freezer, this was a machine with a belt running around inside, in a spiral form so that products came in and spent anything up to an hour in there, continuously moving around before emerging on the same conveyor belt. Freezers ice up, but this unit had a clever trick up its sleeve. It had several sets of cooling coils, but at any one time, one of the coils was being defrosted. It's a bit more technical than that but it is boring enough already.

I travelled to Belgium with an important American customer to show him this marvellous innovation. We arrived at the factory and were greeted by a small Belgian who spoke Dutch and English, but not French. This was apparently much to the disgust of the vast majority of the workforce, who were French speaking. We donned freezer jackets and entered the machine. Anyone who has ever been inside one of these machines, which are running at -40 degrees C with a howling gale blowing around will know that you do not stay inside for long. The first inhale makes your nose hair freeze, and your ears and nose end become icy cold in less than a minute. We saw what we needed to and made our way back to the door. The result of months of continuous operation had meant that the release catch on the inside of the door was a solid block of ice.

The little Belgian was clearly not ready to meet his maker and went immediately into panic mode. He shot across to one of the small openings where the conveyor entered the freezer and started to bellow through the gap. *"Help! Help! We cannot get out. Shit. Shit. Help! Help!"* One of the French speaking operatives was about ten feet from the opening, he didn't flinch, or look around to see where the noise came from. Clearly this guy was a waiter in a French restaurant on an evening and was therefore prepared to ignore anything not communicated in French, no matter how urgent! *"Help! Help! Shit. We are going to die!"* He continued to no avail. The American looked a little concerned but said nothing.

I didn't relish the idea of slowly freezing to death and by now I had a plan and two back up plans. Firstly I was going to try kicking the door open, my plan 'B' was to keep stopping the machine, which would certainly bring the engineers around. Plan 'C' was to shove someone through the mouth opening where the conveyor passed through. I looked at the American, who was a typical American sized kind of fellow, and then down at my own rotund form. It would have to be the little Belgian guy, but I would have to catch him first as by now he was running around like the proverbial headless chicken, bouncing off the walls. Once out through the mouth opening he could hopefully let us out and then lamp the French waiter.

Luckily my first kick at the door did the trick. The door flew open with such force that as it slammed back against the outside wall of the freezer, it left an imprint of the door handle about half an inch deep. The little

Belgian was out before the rest of us, despite having to travel about 15 yards from his position at the other side of the freezer.

The Belgian guy set an engineer on with the task of breaking the ice off the release handle immediately. The American was impressed enough to buy a machine. That night the American and I had a meal in the hotel restaurant and bought a bottle of red wine. The American took a small sip and declared that he didn't like it. We ate up, I drank up, finishing the wine, and then the American declared his intention to get some kip. It was now my turn to bounce off the walls because when I followed about two minutes later I completely misjudged the position of the door out of the dining room and walked into the wall. Even in this state my first reaction was to look around at the remaining diners to see if anyone had seen. They hadn't. Altogether an excellent day out!

23
Hospital

I cannot say that I have been in hospital frequently, although, like a good many people, I have had to have the odd operation, anything from the repair of a stomach hernia, to the removal of a cyst. I have to say that not everything always goes to plan, but so far I have managed to survive everything that the surgeon has attempted, and I have found that this does help somewhat when you come to write about it.

I had to have a minor operation to have four cysts removed from my head, they were just about visible through my thinning hair and just about starting to become a nuisance when I combed my hair. We have a wonderful little Hospital in Otley, and I chose to have this minor procedure done as a day case there. This meant that I would have a local anaesthetic and be fully conscious throughout the operation. There was a small ward with about half a dozen beds, all laid out ready to take what remained of you when the surgeon had cut away your unwanted bits.

My time eventually came and as I walked through from the ward to the theatre, I could not decide which was the worst, the extreme apprehension of being a local anaesthetic virgin, or the fact that I was showing the crack of my butt to the world through the worst theatre-gown-tying-up-job ever!

The surgeon quickly put my mind at rest by asking me what music I would prefer as I climbed up on to the table. Abide With Me came to mind but I decided to leave the choice to the guy with the knife. I certainly didn't want to upset him.

Things that I couldn't see were starting to happen just a couple of inches above my eye-line. Needles, scissors, razor blades were all used and discarded, then came the scalpel. I was aware of tugging and dragging of my scalp but not of any cutting. Seconds later the surgeon announced "one down, three to go". This didn't seem too bad. I decided to pluck up the courage to ask what it was he was removing from my strangely bumpy scalp. He described it as similar to a white baked bean, and showed me the next one that came out, he was right, just like the lumps you get in cottage cheese!

After the operation you get to lounge about in the ward for an hour or two, and eventually a cup of tea is provided for the now starving victims of the surgeon's knife. Before the biscuits arrived I described this white baked bean that the surgeon had shown me to the gent in the next bed. He said that on a previous occasion he had had quite a large cyst removed that had managed to grow in the middle of his chest. This one was like a miniature brain in appearance, about the size of a golf ball. I started to feel queezy. I was informed that he was given the offending appendage to keep as a souvenir, and that he had taken it to work to show them what had been in his lump, whereupon one of his work colleagues put the thing in his mouth for a bet. I didn't eat my biscuits.

After a pleasant rest, I was given my freedom. I had arranged to be picked up by Jackie, who was keeping her mum company at home. Her mum only lives about three hundred yards from the Hospital and it was way before the allotted time for my lift, so I walked. Happy at my survival, I wished everyone I saw along the short walk a good afternoon, only to be greeted with stares and the occasional tentative sounding reply. I began to wonder just what the heck was wrong with people. As I walked up the drive at Jackie's mum's, I caught sight of the reflection of myself in the window. My hair was stuck together in bloodied fingers poking straight out from my head, and between the crusty spikes were bald patches, each with a row of stitching to repair the cut where my baked beans had been removed. I looked like I had survived going head first through a car windscreen, I certainly didn't look up to walking the streets!

Local anaesthetics are not always the best thing where operations are concerned, but general anaesthetics can cause unexpected results, as I found out. At least I think it was the anaesthetic, it could have been a pain thing. I had to have an operation on a stomach hernia, but at the same time, I had an operation on a swelling on one of my testicles. When I came around from my operation I was in some pain and I was connected by a tube (which entered my body close to my appendix) to a large glass vacuum bottle, which was draining fluid from my unfortunate nether regions.

My first meal after the operation was, for the large part, pushed around my plate, and during the visiting time which followed very shortly afterwards I started to feel increasingly grotty, so much so that I asked Jackie to get one of those cardboard tray things that you can puke into. Sometimes these things come over you very quickly and before a suitable receptacle had been obtained, I had to grab the nearest thing to hand, which was a glass urine bottle. I didn't have time to consider its previous usage, or whether it was suitably clean as I pursed my lips in a bizarre sort of a kiss in order to hurl the entire contents of my stomach, diced carrots and all, down the narrow neck of this receptacle. I was proud of the fact that I had achieved this task without spilling a drop, particularly as the ward was full of visitors at the time. The nurse turned up with the cardboard tray and gave me a disbelieving look as I presented her with the steaming bottle of honk in exchange.

I was soon up and about, but still attached to the drain bottle which obviously had to go everywhere with me. This included the loo, where it sat on the floor at the side of me, and the washroom where I chose to stand it on the ledge at the back of the washbasin, in the little soap recess. The unfortunate thing was that I forgot about the fact that this was attached with a bit of tube, and I caught this attachment with my hand as I reached for the towel. The bottle dropped into the washbasin and exploded with an enormous bang into thousands of little polygonal lumps of glass. Before the thought "bollocks" had faded from my head, I was surrounded by nurses, who enquired after me in a concerned way, but at the same time didn't seem to be too pleased about the fact that I had coated myself and their washroom with a mixture of broken glass and the bloody results of having a drain coming from the bottom of my scrotum.

A new drain bottle was quickly organised and connected up. This one was a thick plastic unit. The nurse demonstrated the indestructibility of this replacement unit by rapping me over the knuckles with it!

24
Weddings

Wedding cakes are marvellous things and a sort of a symbol that something really important is happening. This results in a mixture of baking expertise, art and structural engineering, although the latter of these three seems to often be the one that is generally given less than an adequate dose of thinking about. Becky and Mick's cake was a prime example. Even before it came to the point of ceremoniously cutting the cake, one of the pillars had broken through the icing of the bottom layer, and the two upper tiers were starting to lean alarmingly. The cake was on a stand, on a stage behind the head table, and was therefore about five feet above our heads and if I seemed a little preoccupied during the customary speeches, it was the fear that at any moment, Mick and Becky would be decorated with falling cake. As it turned out they never made it on to 'You've Been Framed' wearing the top two tiers, but as they sank the knife in to cut the cake, it went, slowly its angle to the vertical increased until the whole thing dismantled itself a tier at a time. I was still below, and I managed to catch the falling confection without causing too much damage to it or my suit. There was still plenty of cake for everyone else when I had finished juggling with it.

When things like Christenings and weddings come around there are always dilemmas that have to be resolved, for example, who do you have as Godparents and who do you invite to be bridesmaids. It was the second one of these that caused Pollyanne to invite all her daughter and all her nieces to be bridesmaids and that way none of them would be upset because they had been left out. This meant that we had no less than twelve bridesmaids to organise dresses for.

Even transport became a problem and we decided to hire a minibus for the day, which would take the bridesmaids down to the church, and also be able to provide transport to the reception, and back home for anyone who required it. Dee, one of the bridesmaids, who was six at the time of the wedding had tragically lost both legs due to meningitis when she was younger but was determined to stand for the service rather than sit in a wheelchair, her determination made us all very proud of her!

Becky made the cake which was a tower of sponges, covered in butter cream and then decorated with over three hundred fondant icing roses, in a colour scheme which matched the Bridesmaids outfits. Making the roses turned out to be a massive task and we all mucked in to get the required overall covering. The result was wonderful, but extremely heavy.

The day before the wedding we organised to take this marvellous culinary construction up to the hotel where the reception was to be. When we got there it was clear that something was amiss with the cake. The once symmetrical tower was now starting to resemble the tower of Pisa. Something had to be done. I had a piece of bamboo cane in the car, which I chopped off to the right length and with the back edge of an axe [don't ask] I drove it from the top of the cake into the cake-board underneath. It seemed to hold the cake straight. I was concerned that if I had to go to the extent of using guy ropes that someone might notice, and in any case I would have to knock tent pegs into the table top. I hope no one got splinters.

The following morning was a logistical nightmare with everyone except Ian (the groom) getting ready at our house. A car had been organised for Pollyanne, and

Tim had offered to drive the minibus. Eventually the time came and the bride and all the bridesmaids were ready. I have to say, they all looked wonderful. The car and the minibus arrived at the church together and there was the usual gathering of old ladies and other well wishers gathered at the bottom of the Churchyard, eager to see the bride and her attendants. Pollyanne and I got out of the car and waited surrounded by the enthusiastic throng as one by one the bridesmaids got out of the minibus, leaving only Dee to sort out. Tim picked her up to help her down the steps and caught the narrow door frame of the minibus with one of her false legs which then fell off and bounced unceremoniously on to the path in front of the gathered spectators. Completely unperturbed by this, she shouted across to her mum who was watching from the sidelines. *"**Mum! Me leg's come off!**"*

One of the old ladies went a grey colour and shot off up Church Lane like a rat up a drainpipe, another looked as if she was going to faint on the spot and most of the rest stood open mouthed as if they were in shock, I felt like I should be making them a nice sweet cup of tea, and offering trauma counselling. Those of us in the know, particularly Dee thought it was funny but I have to say, there really are times when you know that you shouldn't laugh about something but the something in question keeps coming into your mind in a totally random sort of way, resulting in anything from a sneaky, wry smile to an uncontrollable short burst of air through the laughing gear. I don't think I need to explain.

Lightning Source UK Ltd.
Milton Keynes UK
UKOW03f0323151014

240119UK00001B/4/P